BUS

**ACPL ITEM
DISCARDED**

1/10/08

THE BOSS FROM
OUTER SPACE

AND OTHER ALIENS AT WORK

D1113117

THE BOSS FROM
OUTER SPACE

AND OTHER ALIENS AT WORK

*A Down-to-Earth Guide for Getting Along with
Just About Anyone*

Patricia J. Addesso, Ph.D.

AMACOM

American Management Association
New York * Brussels * Chicago * Mexico City * San Francisco
Shanghai * Tokyo * Washington, D.C.

Special discounts on bulk quantities of AMACOM books are available to corporations, professional associations, and other organizations. For details, contact Special Sales Department, AMACOM, a division of American Management Association, 1601 Broadway, New York, NY 10019.
Tel.: 212-903-8316. Fax: 212-903-8083.
E-mail: specialsls@amanet.org
Website: www.amacombooks.org/go/specialsales
To view all AMACOM titles, go to: www.amacombooks.org

This publication is designed to provide accurate and authoritative information in regard to the subject matter covered. It is sold with the understanding that the publisher is not engaged in rendering legal, accounting, or other professional service. If legal advice or other expert assistance is required, the services of a competent professional person should be sought.

Library of Congress Cataloging-in-Publication Data

Addesso, Patricia J.
    The boss from outer space and other aliens at work : a down-to-earth guide for getting along with just about anyone / Patricia J. Addesso.—1st ed.
        p.   cm.
    Includes index.
    ISBN-13: 978-0-8144-7443-3
    ISBN-10: 0-8144-7443-8
    1. Office politics.   2. Personality.   3. Interpersonal relations.   4. Conflict management.   5. Emotional intelligence.   I. Title.

    HF5386.5.A33   2007
    650.1′3—dc22

                                                                    2007020569

© 2007 Patricia Addesso.
All rights reserved.
Printed in the United States of America.

This publication may not be reproduced,
stored in a retrieval system,
or transmitted in whole or in part,
in any form or by any means, electronic,
mechanical, photocopying, recording, or otherwise,
without the prior written permission of AMACOM,
a division of American Management Association,
1601 Broadway, New York, NY 10019.

Printing number

10   9   8   7   6   5   4   3   2   1

Contents

THE BOSS FROM OUTER SPACE

AND OTHER ALIENS AT WORK

 **Introduction**

To be happier, more successful, and more stress-free at work, you only have to do two things well. Sounds pretty simple, doesn't it? You have to get the job done, and you have to handle the relationships with the people around you. Getting the job done tends to be the easy part. Most of us are trained for that; we went to school, or took classes, or received training once we were hired. But to handle a demanding boss, deal with difficult co-workers or clients, or manage employees who squabble like children—those are the kinds of things that make a job stressful, demanding, and sometimes impossible.

We have always been interested in what makes other people tick; we have just not always been very good at figuring it out. We have all had bosses, co-workers, employees, and customers who sometimes seem like alien beings (not to mention neighbors and family members, but that is a different book). How can we explain it? Is it gender, age differences, astrological signs, cultural differences, or possibly even brain disorders?

Let's flash back several thousand years.

The Place: Ancient China

The Scene: A young man argues for his choice of prospective bride in the face of parental opposition. "No, my son," says his father kindly but firmly. "You know you may not marry a woman born in the year of the snake. She will bring you nothing but misery." Because, of course, everyone knows that you can tell a lot about people by the year in which they were born.

The early Chinese developed a calendar with twelve months based on the moon cycles. They named the years in a cycle of twelve as well, using the names of animals (rat, ox, tiger, etc.). They believed that many of people's characteristics were determined by the year of their births. Females born in the year of the snake, for example, were believed to be so unlucky that they were unlikely to find husbands. Men or women born in the year of the monkey, on the other hand, were considered to be intelligent, were well-liked, and were expected to be successful in life.

The Place: Ancient Greece

The Scene: An angry man shouts at the patrons in his small shop. "Clearly the man is choleric," says a bystander. His behavior, in other words, was explained by the presence of yellow bile in his system.

The ancient Greeks attempted to explain differences among people by classifying them according to which of the four bodily fluids was most prevalent. The sturdy, cheerful, confident, optimistic person was described as sanguine and was believed to have these characteristics because blood was the predominant body fluid. A person with too much phlegm was "phlegmatic": impassive, slow, and stolid. The melancholic person had a lot of black bile and was described as depressed, sad, and dejected. Too much yellow bile led to a person being hot-tempered and angry, or choleric.

Now let's fast forward.

The Place: The United States, 1973

The Scene: A disco bar. A young man with a heavy gold chain around his neck comes closer. I can see now that there is a zodiac figure suspended from the chain: two small naked cherubs—the "twin" sign, or Gemini. He gets close enough to see the stylized lion hanging from my own, thinner chain, indicating Leo, of course. Obviously not too observant, he leers, "What's your sign?"

We make some assumptions on our compatibility, or lack thereof, based on the jewelry (in my case, probably influenced by the leer and the stupid pickup line). Have we come a long way, or not?

Astrology is built on the idea that the position of the stars and planets at the time of our births determines many of the differences among people. The year is divided into 12 sections, called the zodiac, which correspond to 12 constellations that lay across the sky. Each constellation is regarded as the house of a particular planet, and the position of the sun in the constellation at the moment of our birth is regarded as having an impact on our personality. Thus we have the flamboyant Leo or the stolid Taurus.

The Place: Corporate America, the 1990s

The Scene: Yet another diversity workshop. "Welcome," beams the trainer. "We are here to learn about one another's cultural backgrounds and learn to truly value diversity in all forms, including sexual preference, age, and ethnicity."

"Not to mention gender," says a participant, not lifting her head from a copy of *Men are from Mars, Women are from Venus.*[1]

"What about birth order?" asks another, waving his copy of *The Birth Order Factor.*[2]

So more recently, we have looked at differences in gender, race, sexual preference, birth order, and age to categorize and deal with our differences. Men and women, for example, are characterized as having different communication styles. The trouble is, some men communicate more like women, and vice versa. First-borns are "known" to be aggressive go-getters, more likely to be corporation presidents or millionaires. Of course, there are a whole lot of first-borns who are neither! Employers have shown a great deal of interest these days in helping us get along with our co-workers in the face of diversity. Corporations offer workshops in dealing with people of different ethnic and cultural backgrounds.

Where do we stand today? From the brief examples above you can see that people have always been fascinated by the differences among themselves, trying to explain them and trying to get along with others. From astrology to birth order to gender, in different eras we have called on different explanations of why other people are different from us. The goal of all of these explanations is a better understanding of how we can learn to get along with other people despite our differences. These differences can lead to conflict or, if managed properly, to a greater appreciation of other people. In fact, people who look at things differently than we do are very valuable to us, as long as we don't get so annoyed that we avoid them.

The premise of all of these efforts is that if we understand someone who is different from us, we can communicate with that person more effectively, and thus we can live and work with that person more effectively. The premise of this book is that none of these efforts go far enough—that people will not truly value differences until they recognize and value different personality traits, cognitive styles, and communication styles. There are quite a few of these kinds of factors that we may not even be aware of, but that have a huge impact on our ability to get along with other people. For now I will refer to these factors as "personality" for the sake of convenience, although they are not all strictly personality traits.

Personality is the invisible diversity. It is the factor that causes you to get along great with some people while other people annoy you. You may meet someone of the same age, race, and gender as yourself, only to find that you can't communicate at all. I know I have met people who look just like me but are clearly from another planet. One basic human tendency is to assume that we are normal and that everyone else should be like us. That is, of course, not true. We will live, work, play, and love more happily if we understand that every other person is somewhat different than we are. The more different a person is, the more she may annoy us, but the more we really need her to round out our view of the world. Think about a work team in which all the members think alike. They will work together very smoothly, but they may not be as effective as a team that experiences conflict once in a while in ways that get the creative juices flowing. There are strengths and weaknesses to be found in every personality type, if we just know where to look.

THE RESEARCH

The personality traits, cognitive styles, and communication styles that I am going to talk about in this book are based on several traditions of research. If you are the type of reader who is not interested in these things, feel free to skip to the end of this introduction and read the last several paragraphs. Otherwise, follow me on this brief journey through the many years of research that have led us to this point. I am going to talk about the personality research that culminated in a consensus around what are called the "Big Five" personality factors, the characteristics of human temperament that we can trace back to the work of Carl Jung, emotional intelligence, differences in cognitive style, differences in activity level, and differences in motivational needs.

THE BIG FIVE

Let's begin with the Big Five factors of personality. Many researchers have identified hundreds of bundles of personality traits, but after many years and literally hundreds of research studies there is now substantial consensus around the five traits that can most efficiently describe a person.[3] These five show up across cultures as well.[4] The five are:

1. Extroversion

2. Agreeableness

3. Conscientiousness

4. Emotional stability

5. Openness to experience

Extroversion is one of the most readily observable personality traits. Most of us are fairly good at making judgments about whether other people are introverts or extroverts. We experience people as either talkative or quiet. We may find them sociable, outgoing, and open, or quiet loners. Extroverts think by talking, and much of what they say (in work meetings, for example) involves thinking out loud. Introverts think by mulling things over and need time and solitude to do so.

As far as *agreeableness* goes, people will fall somewhere on a continuum from cooperative and good natured to irritable and negative. You may be wondering about the strengths and weaknesses in this case. What's wrong with being agreeable? The obvious weakness with extreme agreeableness is an inability to stand up for oneself or buck the tide of popular opinion. Being too good-natured, too mild, too cooperative—you can see that these drawbacks are almost as big as being too negative, too uncooperative, or too irritable. Agreeableness influences how you communicate with people. At one end of the spectrum you will find the very direct, open, and honest person. At the other end is the tactful, diplomatic soul. Either person can be very useful to you, or very annoying.

The third of the Big Five personality traits is called *conscientiousness*. This trait compares the responsible, fussy, persevering person with the careless, undependable, flexible person. Once again, as we saw in previous traits, people on either end of the spectrum have their good points and their bad, and they may cause difficulties in organizations. A person who is too conscientious may be a real barrier to rapid change and getting things done. A perfectionist may spend all of his time and energy planning, not doing. The careless person may be of more assistance to you when you have a project that needs to get done quickly—not perfectly, but quickly.

The fourth of the Big Five personality traits is *emotional stability*. At one end of the continuum we find the very calm, composed, and poised individual. At the other end is the very nervous, anxious, and excitable person. As with the other traits, there is no "good" place to be on this continuum. There are benefits to both types. So how could there possibly be benefits to being nervous and anxious? It is probably less clear than with the other traits, but there are times that a nervous, excitable person may be just what you need. He may bring needed energy to a project. A person with a lot of nervous energy may not do well with a task that requires concentrated desk time, and on the other hand, the calm, composed employee may not seem to have the sense of urgency that the project or job demands. She is too mellow; she may not seem to care too much about the job or task at hand.

The last of the Big Five personality traits is called *openness to experience*. The trait is also called *culture* or *sophistication*. The fact that this trait has three names, and that researchers have not been able to agree on just what it should be called, is your first clue that this is a complicated one. At one end of the spectrum we have people who are intellectual, artistically sensitive, polished, refined, and imaginative. Some adjectives that have been used to describe the other end of the continuum are artistically insensitive, unreflective, narrow, and direct. There is a great deal of snobbery evident in these adjectives and certainly in the understanding of these personality types in the workplace.

An open person is more self-reflective and thinks about her own personality and the effect it has on other people. None of us likes to number ourselves among the narrow-minded people we know. The fact is, too many of us are. This trait is not related to intelligence. There are very smart people who are not very open to new ideas, and less smart people who are. People who are high on this trait tend to be open to new data as it comes in, even after they have made a decision. People who are low on this trait tend to see things in a more black-and-white fashion ("I have made up my mind. Now let's move on."). When confronted with someone who disagrees with them, people who are high on this trait tend to say something like, "Isn't that interesting? Why do you think so?" People who are low on this trait are more abrupt: "You're wrong."

TEMPERAMENT

In addition to the Big Five model, there are some interesting twists brought to our understanding of human behavior by the temperament research of Carl Jung.[5] Although not as widely researched as the Big Five, various instruments that measure these temperament factors are widely used and certainly affect the workplace.[6] Let's explore these factors next.

The Jungian research places human temperament along four continuums:

1. Extroverted (E), Introverted (I)

2. Sensing (S), Intuitive (N)

3. Thinking (T), Feeling (F)

4. Judging (J), Perceiving (P)

The first dimension, represented by the letters E and I, characterizes people as either extroverted or introverted. This is similar to the Big Five personality trait of extroversion, but the temperament research defines it a bit differently. In the temperament research, we are talking more about where people get their energy. Extroverted people derive their energy from the outside world of other people, but introverted people gain strength from their internal thoughts and ideas. Extroverted people appear at ease while socializing, being gregarious, conversing with strangers, and thinking out loud. This creates energy for them. The introverted personality is less approachable, decides matters and speaks up more slowly, and prefers quiet and being away from a crowd. Socializing and being gregarious actually drains energy from an introvert. Extroverted personalities in the workplace are better suited for tasks requiring social contact and communication. Introverted personalities are a better fit for jobs like data analysis, strategizing, and organizing.

The second dimension is intuition versus sensing. This trait describes how people prefer to collect information. Intuitive personalities like to get information subjectively and intuitively, usually without a formal system. In contrast, sensing personalities prefer to collect factual information systematically, based on the five senses (they like things they can see and touch, for example). Intuitive types prefer to get the overall picture of an experience, but the sensing type prefers to have the details. The intuitive personalities would be a good fit for jobs requiring innovation, creativity, conceptualization, and vision. Sensing personalities fit better with quantitative data analysis, practical and specific tasks, and jobs that call upon their sense of orderliness.

Thinking versus feeling is the third temperament dimension. This dimension identifies the way in which people make decisions. Thinking people prefer to use logic and facts to decide, but feeling personalities prefer to focus on how people will feel about and be affected by the decision. Thinking types use cause-and-effect reasoning and the scientific method to consider the evidence objectively without emotional involvement. Feeling types weigh the options against their personal values more than their rational logic. People in the thinking category tend to be analytical, critical, impersonal, and objective. Their preference is for the "bottom line" logic and rationale. People in the feeling end of the dimension show more empathy and appreciation, use their hearts rather than their heads to consider implications, are much more likely to consider the human values, and prefer to be personal and subjective in the decision-making process.

The perceiving versus judging dimension refers to how much information a person requires before feeling comfortable in making a decision. Those in the judging category prefer to make decisions and resolve problems quickly. At the opposite end of the spectrum, perceiving people prefer to be adaptable to events and flexible enough to keep their options open. Judging types work hard to get closure on issues. They like to be decisive and methodical, prefer minimal information on which to base their decisions, and tend to get nervous when a decision is still on the table ("Let's make up our mind already!"). Perceivers are more curious and spontaneous, prefer to collect as much information as possible to make a decision, and like having options. In this way, perceivers are better at collecting and analyzing data, but they may hesitate too long in deciding and taking action.

EMOTIONAL INTELLIGENCE

One of the things that causes people's behaviors and reactions to differ in the workplace is the degree to which they are emotionally intelligent. There is a body of knowledge and research available to us on emotional intelligence, sparked by an author named Daniel Goleman.[7] He followed up his initial work with some information on how this trait influences us in the workplace.[8] His basic premise is that intelligence, or IQ, is not always as important as emotional intelligence, or what he calls EQ. Emotional intelligence has the following components:

- Self-awareness

- Impulse control

- Persistence

- Self-motivation

- Empathy

- Social deftness

Although the original research looked at people in life and in relationships, these factors are also very important in the workplace. Lack of emotional intelligence can get in the way of a good career and cause people to fail. Essentially, an emotionally intelligent person does not always act on her emotional impulses. She is able to read what another person is feeling and can handle relationships smoothly.

Self-awareness refers to the ability to monitor and understand yourself. When you are too angry to speak with someone, you tell him so and reschedule the meeting rather than scream at him and have an unproductive conversation. Self-aware people recognize their emotions as well as their strengths and weaknesses. They know what their hot buttons are and what impact other people's moods may have on them. They understand their own motivations, goals, and values. The most important thing to understand about self-awareness is that it is a very realistic assessment of oneself. It is neither overly critical nor overly optimistic.

Emotionally intelligent people are able to control their impulses and their moods. They think before they act and are not carried away by their impulses. They tend to act appropriately in any given situation. These people do get into bad moods and feel emotional impulses just like everyone else does. Basically,

3 1833 05388 3341

the difference is that they can choose when to act on their emotions and when not to. Usually these people get a reputation for fairness and integrity.

Emotionally intelligent people are not easily discouraged. They are not pessimistic and do not easily give up. They have a healthy self-confidence and believe in their ability to succeed.

Emotionally intelligent people work for reasons beyond simply making a paycheck. They tend to motivate themselves, finding internal satisfaction in what they do. They do not look to other people for praise, criticism, or rewards—or at least they do these things to a lesser extent than other people.

Emotionally intelligent people are tapped into the emotional states of other people. They not only notice emotions in other people, they are usually fairly accurate in assessing it. Empathy allows them to consider other people's feelings in a thoughtful manner. Keep in mind that it does not mean that they agree with other people all the time or that they try to please everybody.

All in all, emotionally intelligent people can deal with other people in any given social situation. They have class and poise. They do not come across as rude, brash, or inappropriate. Socially skilled people work in teams well and find it easy to persuade others to see their perspectives. Obviously, an ability to manage relationships can only be helpful in the workplace.

COGNITIVE STYLE

People who simply think differently than we do are interesting to have around. They can either cause us to see things differently and thus be valuable to us or become so annoying that we avoid them. The particular cognitive style that seems to cause the most difficulty at work, and the one we are going to concentrate on in this book, is the style that causes some people to be very detail-oriented and others to take a more global or conceptual look at the world around them.[9]

The people who think globally or about the big picture like to start with a general understanding of the task at hand, but the detail-oriented people prefer to start with a more structured step-by-step approach. So you can see that there is potential for conflict right from the start of a task or project. As I have said about the other personality traits, there are strengths and weaknesses to both approaches. The best teams have both types of people so that they can draw on the strengths of both.

ACTION ORIENTATION

Another trait that can cause people to behave and react differently at work is their physical energy level. Some people are simply more active than others. The psychological community refers to the extreme ends of this continuum as mania and depression. People who swing back and forth between the extremes may suffer from bipolar disorder or manic depression. In this book, I am talking about normal variations in energy level. Someone with a high level of energy, but still within the normal level, is sometimes referred to as hypomanic, and there is some evidence that he or she is valuable to have around in the workplace.[10]

Hypomania refers to a person who tends to have a lot of energy, likes to keep active, is usually in a good mood, etc. Of course, as you may have guessed, I will make a case for the person of lower energy being just as valuable in his own right. Someone who is very active may move a little too quickly, and her decisions and judgments may be impaired to some degree by that quick action. She may benefit from having a lower-energy person on her team to slow her down.

MOTIVATIONAL NEEDS

A motivational researcher named David McClelland[11] tells us that three needs create different types of motivations and behaviors in the workplace: power, achievement, and affiliation. To understand the idea, think about a pie chart divided into thirds. You are the pie and you are made up of these three needs (power, achievement, and affiliation). Each person's pie chart looks a little (or a lot) different.

There could conceivably be an individual whose pie chart was divided into three evenly sized slices. Most often, however, one of the three seems to take precedence. The largest is the factor that has an influence on how we behave at work and of course in the rest of our lives as well.

The person for whom power is the largest slice of his pie wants to have an influence on what's going on around him. He has a strong need to be a leader and for his team or co-workers to accept his ideas. He enjoys having status and status symbols. He responds well to praise and enjoys prestige.

Let's look at an example. Cindy has a lot of need for power, some need for achievement, and very little need for affiliation. She is liable to be very successful as a manager in a hierarchical organization such as the military. She likes to be in control and is mostly motivated by a drive to take charge. She is not overly concerned about whether people like her or not, so she is able to make tough and unpopular decisions.

People whose largest slice of the pie is the need for achievement are motivated largely by a sense of accomplishment. Achievement is their largest incentive in life. They need goals, and they need to see advancement toward those goals. They need feedback as to how they are advancing.

Consider Juan. Juan has a large need for achievement. He has a little need for affiliation and very little need for power. He is very well suited for his job as a research scientist who works in a lab. His motivation is the scientific research that he does and the breakthroughs he makes. He is not interested in managing people or serving on teams.

What about the person whose largest need is affiliation? This person has a need for friendly relationships, and her motivation is interaction with other people. This person is the quintessential team player. She needs to be liked and will be the one who is always checking in with the others and making sure that everyone is okay with decisions, that everyone has been heard, and that everyone is willing to move forward.

Brooke has a lot of need for affiliation, some need for power, and little need for achievement. She needs to be around people a lot, so her job as a customer service representative for a utility company is perfect for her. She never wants to go into management. She needs supervision from her boss, though, in the form of clear goals to strive for and clear reward systems.

ELEVEN TYPES REVOLVING AROUND ONE ANOTHER

How does the research above fit into the eleven personality traits, cognitive styles, and communication styles in the rest of the book? There is not a one-to-one fit; the eleven types are somewhat influenced by one another. For example, someone with a high need for power will act a bit differently if he is also emotionally intelligent versus if he is not. As I began to ponder this book, I began to think of it in bottom-line, practical terms. What are the things that cause conflict at work? What causes problems among co-workers, between employees and their bosses, and between bosses and their employees?

I entered the workplace at the age of 17, bagging groceries in a supermarket. I studied psychology in college, studied industrial psychology in graduate school, was a manager in three different organizations, and since 1995 have been a consultant to organizations and an executive coach. Essentially, since I was 17 I have been observing what people tend to call "personality conflicts" at work, and when this book began to take form in my mind it occurred to me that these eleven types seemed to emerge over and over in every industry I have worked with and at every level, from entry-level employee to CEO. So it seemed most helpful to outline these traits for you and share with you how best to deal with the inevitable fallout when these types clash in the workplace. The eleven personality types described in this book are based on a combination of the research I described earlier and my own years of observation. The terms I use to describe the types are my own.

People have a lot of stress and even leave jobs over troubles with their co-workers or "personality conflicts" with their bosses, and managers have been known to accept demotions voluntarily so that they do not have to deal with employees anymore. As they say, "Management would be easy if it weren't for the people."[12]

Think of a bell-shaped curve and a characteristic like height. There is a small percentage of people in this world who are extremely tall, and a small percentage of people who are extremely short. The closer we get to average height, the more people you find in that category. The same is true of the characteristics described in this book. Most of you will probably be average on many of them but will find that you are either high or low on several others. Those are the ones that you will want to pay the most attention to because those are the ones that tend to cause you difficulty at work. If you are low on a particular characteristic, there are certain attitudes and behaviors that accompany that characteristic. Those attitudes and behaviors may feel very normal to you, but they cause conflict with the people around you that are medium or high on that characteristic.

The "Before We Travel" section of each chapter tells you what type of research each characteristic is based on, but how do you know if you are high, medium, or low in that characteristic? I hesitate to refer you to specific Web sites because those tend to come and go. But there are places on the Internet where you can take quick quizzes to get a sense of your placement on many of these characteristics. Before you read the rest of this book, you may want to put the following search terms into an Internet search engine:

- Big Five personality test

- Emotional intelligence quiz

- Jungian temperament sorter

- McClelland's motivators test

- Learning style test

We will look at eleven different personality traits, cognitive styles, and communication styles and the ways that they can cause conflict at work. Because I like the way these traits make a person at one extreme appear so "alien" to a person at the other extreme, and because I wanted an overall framework to work within, I will use the planets as a unifying metaphor. (I'm using the sun and the moon to make up the numbers, and yes, I know Pluto was demoted in late 2006—for good reason when you see what personality characteristic it is associated with.) There is no underlying reason for using these designations. I am simply having some fun pulling together a complex set of personality traits.

I will look at extremes of each trait (the person who is "high" and the person who is "low") to make the point. Keep in mind that there are also many people who fall somewhere in between (the "balanced" individuals). We will look at characteristics of a person high on each trait, low on each trait, the other possible combinations, and the ramifications of mixing different traits among bosses, employees, and co-workers. I end each chapter with some tips on how to be more balanced and I include reminders of what to expect from the people of various types.

CHAPTER 1
Co-Workers from the Sun

The sun! Hard to imagine life without it, isn't it? In fact, there would be no life without it; it is warm, nurturing, and life-giving. Of course, it would kill us if we could not get away from it from time to time; the shadow is a cool and refreshing change of pace. Nightfall is a natural and necessary counterpart to the sunny day. And just as we cannot live our lives only in the sunshine, if we lived only in the dark, we would soon die as well. A theme we will see over and over in this book is that it is essential to strike a balance between two extremes, even if we have a preference for one over the other.

THE LIFE OF THE PARTY/THE QUIET ONE

Do you have two (or more) co-workers? Then chances are good that you have had experience dealing with the two types I am going to discuss in this chapter. One extreme here is the intro-vert: a *reserved, quiet, self-sufficient* person—the kind who stays in the shadows, out of the light. The other extreme is the extro-vert: someone who is *outgoing, sociable, and active*—the "sunny" disposition. Extroverts must shine their personalities in all directions to feel right.

Deciding whether someone is an introvert or an extrovert is probably one of the easier decisions to make about an individual's personality. Many people are clearly extroverts, many are clearly introverts, and, like all of the traits I will be discussing, some people fall somewhere in between on the continuum. Also, like all of the traits I will be discussing, neither is better or worse than the other. What we need to work on is a better understanding of the person we are not—the side that is alien to us. We also need to figure out a way to better balance our own strengths with the strengths of those who are different.

BEFORE WE TRAVEL TO THE SUN

Extroversion, the first of the "Big Five" personality traits (discussed in the introduction), has been widely researched. There is some evidence that this trait is to some degree biologically determined. Parents of very young children have noticed that some are very outgoing and others shrink from loud noises and contact from strangers. Introverts may simply be born more sensitive to sensory input, so they protect themselves from too much noise, too many people, and too much of any kind of input. An extroverted baby will show interest in a noisy toy; an introverted baby may cry and cover her ears. The basic definition of introverts is that they are oriented toward the inner world of ideas, and the basic definition of extroverts is that they are oriented toward the outer world of people. As a result, we end up with this state of affairs in the workplace: Extroverts get their energy from other people, and introverts get their energy from their own ideas.

To further complicate matters, one of the facts of human nature is that we tend to think that we are normal. "Sure," think the extroverts, "we like to seek out other people and brainstorm ideas; isn't that natural? Isn't that the best way to do things?" All the while, our colleague down the hall (the introvert) is thinking, "Sure, I like to go in to my office and shut the door and quietly think about issues that are critical and need to be solved immediately. That is how I do my best work, and it always has been. Doesn't everyone do it that way?" You can see how this can create some tension in the workplace. Our question for this chapter is, How do you deal with these differences?

Once you understand this trait and its complexities, you have a series of decisions to make.

Which End of the Spectrum Most Characterizes Me?

Are you oriented toward other people, or are you oriented inward? How can you assess situations so that you know when (1) you can best use your natural abilities to contribute the most; or (2) you need to "stretch" a bit in the opposite direction because the other type of behavior is needed?

A Little Bit of Sun. If you are an introvert, you can still work on a team, be around other people, be involved in brainstorming, and enter into other extroverted activities. It will simply take some energy rather than be energizing. Rather than doing something that you prefer and that comes naturally, you must sometimes choose behavior that feels a bit unnatural but can become more of a habit over time with some practice.

A Little Bit of Shade. If you are an extrovert, you can still work alone and not annoy the introverts around you by constantly knocking on their doors and asking them if you can "run something by them." It will just take more energy instead of being energizing. It is not natural behavior for you, but it can be a choice. You just need to choose your times wisely and understand who you are dealing with.

Which End of the Spectrum Most Characterizes Those Closest to Me at Work: My Boss, My Co-Workers, My Peers, and My Employees?

How can you best use their natural abilities? How can you avoid expecting them to do things that fly in the face of their natural styles, and how can you stop being disappointed in them or angry at them when they do what just comes naturally to them? When introverts are naturally quiet in a meeting, you can choose to get angry at them, or you can do helpful things like give them the agenda ahead of time to allow them to think through contributions they might wish to make. When extroverts are "shining" all over the place in a meeting and taking up valuable time, you can get them back on track in a tactful way and harness that energy productively. You also need to ask yourself how you can change your own behavior, when appropriate, to get along better with those who are different.

I will revisit these questions in the worksheet at the end of the chapter.

INTROVERTS IN NEED OF THE SUN

Marco and Janet both graduated near the top of their class in chemical engineering. They got their first jobs at a large pharmaceutical company that recruited at their campus, and they found themselves working in a department that reported to the vice president of marketing. After a few months on the job, their boss sent them to their first professional conference, and it was somewhat of a disaster. She expected them to make some connections, network, talk about their company to various other companies in their industry, and arrange some business dinners. Because they were both introverts, they walked around the conference rooms, made eye contact, smiled at people, but with the best of intentions, they spoke to no one! It was probably a combination of their introversion and their recent student status, but they had no luck initiating conversations and had to go back to their boss on Monday morning and admit that their networking plans had failed. Needless to say, their midyear performance reviews, although reflecting good work in the technical side of the job, suffered a bit due to this incident.

At the next year's conference, they brought along a colleague named Susanna. Susanna was highly extroverted. Janet did some research ahead of time, which as an introvert she was very good at and enjoyed. She looked at the list of conference attendees and found out a bit about their backgrounds, both personal and professional. When she saw someone, she would alert Susanna. ("That's Michael Alexander. He had an article in the last issue of *Pharma Update* about new methods of marketing research." Or, "That is Wendy Peterman. She is a VP at Mega-Pharm and gave birth to twins last year.") Susanna, the extrovert, would then approach the person and strike up a conversation based on the information Janet was feeding her. Janet and Marco had no trouble joining a conversation that was already flowing around them when their colleague was in the middle of it, especially because they had done their homework on the people and their backgrounds. The three of them made a great team, and that year they made the connections, did the networking, and had the business dinners.

LET THE SUN SHINE: CHARACTERISTICS OF AN EXTROVERT

Extroverts are outgoing and sociable. They enjoy groups of people, like being on teams or group projects, and enjoy idle chatter. They like to brainstorm ideas when they are trying to think something through.

Extroverts tend to think by talking. They will say things like, "Let me run something by you," or "Let me think out loud a minute." They will often say things they are sorry for later because they speak very spontaneously instead of rehearsing their thoughts ahead of time.

They are good at concentrating despite distractions. They can converse with the TV or radio on, talk on the phone while driving, and have a meaningful conversation at a crowded party.

They approach and are approached by co-workers, strangers, neighbors, and other people more often than introverts. They tend to have a large circle of friends and acquaintances.

STANDING IN THE SHADOWS: CHARACTERISTICS OF AN INTROVERT

Introverts are reserved and quiet. They are more self-sufficient than extroverts and like spending time alone. They like to think things through by themselves before they are called on to offer ideas about something.

To an introvert, saying something like, "I'll think about that and let you know later," is quite legitimate and is not necessarily a delaying tactic. Introverts don't like to think out loud and will have carefully thought out much of what they say. Many of them even rehearse conversations ahead of time to be sure they have the points they want to make straight in their minds.

They enjoy peace and quiet and "down time," and they like time spent alone or in the company of a few close friends or family members.

SOLAR COMBINATIONS

Now let's look at what happens when we combine two extroverts, two introverts, and one of each.

Two Extroverts

These two will have a lot of fun together. Both enjoy activity, conversation, and other people. When working together, they will often be quite productive and come up with a tremendous amount of ideas. In fact, two people may not be enough. Two extroverts may go looking for a team. A team of extroverts can be quite overwhelming to someone observing it from the outside, particularly if that person is not an extrovert. And that takes us to the next subject: the downsides of extroverts working together.

When extroverts work together, they generate a lot of ideas and have a lot of fun. This takes time. One may wonder when the work is going to get done. A serious-minded, introverted boss may look in on an extroverted team and wonder if they are doing any work at all. They are! They are getting work done in their own way. A boss may need to remind them of deadlines, and an extroverted team may need to pay special attention to introverted members who may not be getting any "air time" to state their ideas.

Two Introverts

Put two introverts in a room or on a work team and you will have lots of "quiet time." There are long silences between the two, but they are not uncomfortable silences. They tend to enjoy the same level of noise and activity; that is, a low level.

This duo is not likely to seek out other members. In fact, two may be too many; either one would have probably been just as happy working alone. Remember, introverts are drawn to the inner world of ideas, and each spends quite a bit of time brainstorming in his own brain. Each might be doing a tremendous amount of work—and very good work—alone. And again, of course, that leads us to some downsides.

Introverts are often not given the credit they deserve in teams. They will sit in meetings with a great idea, or even a tremendous amount of ideas, in those brains of theirs. But they either have no way to get the attention of the crowd or no desire to do so. Or perhaps they haven't really fully articulated what they want to say until some time after the meeting. So they meet the boss or the facilitator of the meeting later in the hallway or in the lunchroom and say something like, "I was thinking about what we were saying in that meeting, and here's an idea I had." Now the boss is understandably angry that the person didn't bring up this wonderful idea in the meeting when it could have done some good, even though this is the usual, and even predictable, introvert behavior.

Sometimes the introvert may even have brought up the idea in the meeting but was not heard. An extrovert tends to know how to "get the floor" in a meeting. He shifts his body in the chair, sits up straighter, pulls up to the table, looks around, and signals to the rest of the room that "it is my turn to talk now." Then when he begins to speak, he does not begin with his great idea. He begins with some "throwaway words" just to get the room quiet and to get the attention on himself; perhaps he begins with, "Well, you know, that's a good point, Roger, and that reminds me of something else we might want to think about, so let me run this by you all and see what you think." He will speak for 30 seconds or so without saying anything—long enough for the side conversations in the room to stop and for all eyes in the room to go to him. Then he will come out with his great idea. Introverts, on the other hand, tend simply to state their great idea, which is lost in the babble of the general meeting, and then they are hurt or puzzled when no one remembers they spoke or no one hears them. Or, worse yet, someone

CO-WORKERS FROM THE SUN

else (some extrovert) says the exact same thing 10 or 20 minutes later and everyone says, "Oh, what a great idea!"

One of Each

If the relationship between an introvert and an extrovert is understood and valued, it can be very helpful to both of them (as in our opening case study, when Janet did the background work and Susanna did the social connecting). And that of course is a very big if! We have seen several examples already where people can misunderstand behavior. When introverts and extroverts collide, conflict seems inevitable.

When you put an introvert and an extrovert on a task together, the extrovert will begin talking. She will then stop talking and wait for the introvert to say something. The introvert is still thinking and so may not begin speaking immediately. The extrovert will then talk some more. The extrovert is thinking, "Does this person have nothing of value to add?" The introvert is thinking, "Will this person ever shut up so that I can talk?" What a way to begin a task together, right? Will it go downhill from here? This is certainly not a very auspicious beginning.

Let's look at the scenario a little more carefully. Obviously, the extrovert will speak first. Then she stops talking—in her mind, anyway. That pause, however, probably lasts about two seconds. That isn't nearly long enough for an introvert. An extrovert who knows she's dealing with an introvert has to make a real effort to stop talking for about 10 seconds (and 10 seconds is simply an eternity for an extrovert). An extrovert who knows she's dealing with an introvert also knows a few other tricks. She not only stops talking, she follows up by asking a question, something like, "What do you think?" Then she stops talking again and waits as long as it takes for the answer.

Co-Workers. I worked with a small group once in the training department of a telecommunications company. We all took a personality test and one of the men in the department tested as a high introvert. He seemed somewhat relieved to be able to show the rest of the department his scores. He explained to them why he never went on the 10 A.M. coffee break but went out on the patio instead: "It's not that I don't like you all, it's just that I like going out on the patio by myself."

There are more extroverts in the world than introverts, so introverts tend to be misunderstood. Introverts are not necessarily socially shy or backward. They simply like their own company. They don't wish they were in the crowd, and extroverts aren't necessarily doing them a favor by getting them off of the patio and bringing them in to the coffee break. Go ahead and invite them, but don't insist, and don't feel hurt when they say no. Many introverts I know feel the need to make up politically correct excuses for saying no, particularly on business trips when the days are spent in meetings and the nights are spent at dinners. They want to spend evenings alone in their hotel rooms, but that isn't socially acceptable, so they make up business-related excuses such as "I have so much work to do," "I have so many e-mails to return," or "I have that budget to work on."

If you are an extrovert among introverted co-workers, feel free to invite them to things, but do not feel hurt when they turn you down. Don't look for ulterior motives when they turn down invitations, and don't take it personally. You may want to look for people to go to lunch with in other departments. In meetings, don't be afraid of quiet time. People are thinking. Don't feel the need to fill that time with talk. When you say something and no one responds, it doesn't mean that no one heard you, that no one agrees with you, or that everyone is asleep.

If you are an introvert among extroverted co-workers, accept their invitations once in a while. It is not necessary to join them every time, but do go occasionally. And explain to them that you really like your alone time and you prefer to spend your lunch hour reading your novel on the patio, or returning calls, or shopping, or what ever it is you do. In meetings, try to speak up once in a while. Get the attention of the room first in the ways I talked about in the "Two Introverts" section. If at all possible, get the agenda of the meeting in advance and plan what you're going to say. Script it out if possible, but don't read your script to the audience. Simply rehearse it in your mind so that you know what you want to say and so that you're comfortable when it comes time to speak up in the meeting.

Boss and Employee. The introverted manager can be a challenge to his employees. He is not easy to read. Is he having a good day or a bad day? Is he pleased with your work or annoyed? Because he does not readily say what's on his mind, an employee might be left in the dark. Imagine how frustrating that can be.

One of the things we know about job satisfaction is that it is critical to get feedback on your work. Whether we are doing a good job or whether there's room for improvement, it's important that our boss lets us know one way or the other. The introverted boss, who walks by us without a word, leaves us wondering. I had a colleague once who compared this to bowling with a curtain between the bowlers and the pins. You could throw balls down the alley all night, and you could hear various noises when the pins fell over, but no one kept score and you couldn't see where your pins fell, and it wasn't a whole lot of fun.

We are indebted to two researchers named J. Richard Hackman and Greg Oldham, who came up with what they called the Job Characteristics Model.[1] According to the model, five characteristics need to be present to create job satisfaction.

1. An employee needs to have some variety in the work he does every day (task variety) so that his job does not get monotonous and boring.

2. At the end of the day, he needs to feel like he can look at a whole and complete piece of work, unlike the old assembly line days when an employee simply tightened the seventh bolt on the left and had no idea what the final piece of work was going to look like. This is known as task identity.

3. The employee must feel like his job matters, that it has an impact. This is known as task significance.

4. It is important that the employee feels that he has at least some level of autonomy in deciding how to do the job.

5. Finally, the employee needs feedback. How is he doing: good, bad, or indifferent?

You can see that quite a few of these factors involve the manager communicating clearly to the employee. The introverted manager is at a disadvantage here. The introverted manager needs to make a real effort not only to give the employee feedback regularly, but to instill in the employee a sense of the significance of his job.

I knew a manager once who supervised the custodial staff in a large building. I was talking to him about some of these theories and he said, "My guys don't care about this stuff." I tried to tell him not to underrate his staff. They may be "just the janitors," but there isn't any reason why they can't take pride in their work, see the impact of what they do, and get feedback that will allow them to improve themselves. He had a problem keeping staff; admittedly, the work was not exactly challenging. He would find employees asleep in the janitor's closet, for example. He had a bad habit of keeping to his own office, though, because he was an introvert. He had to make a real effort to instill a sense of pride in his employees, let them see the significance of what they were doing, and give them feedback.

One of the key components of most leadership-development programs is developing people skills. Many managers come up through the ranks from technical areas such as accounting, computer programming, or finance. They need to learn simple people skills like stopping to talk to people in the hallways. These are things that extroverts do naturally and introverts need to learn. Managers do need to be a little bit extroverted for a variety of reasons. Introverts can be good managers, but they need to make that extra effort to learn some extroverted behavior.

If you have an introverted boss, do not hesitate to ask for feedback. Request a meeting, and let her know in advance what it is about. As I have said several times, as with all introverts, give her the agenda ahead of time, don't just start springing questions on her once you get there! Depending upon your job and the pressures of your business, it may not be unreasonable to suggest a weekly, monthly, or quarterly meeting, even if it can only be 15 minutes or so. Negotiate!

Employee and Boss. What about the extroverted boss who needs to deal with introverted employees? This boss has all the people skills he needs. He walks down the hall every morning and says,

"Hey, how's everybody doing?" only to be met with blank stares, perhaps. Or he opens a meeting with, "I'd like to get everyone's thoughts on the new project," and is met with dead silence.

That boss needs to learn to ask questions differently. First thing Monday morning, perhaps he needs to stop at Joe's desk and say, "Joe, how did your son's soccer game go on Saturday?" Joe is an introvert and needs a specific question to respond to. And a day or two before the meeting about the new project, the boss needs to send out an agenda with a notation that he wants everyone's thoughts on the new project and that he's going to begin with that question.

The extroverted boss also needs to think carefully about employee recognition. She may think there is nothing better than gala award ceremonies where employees are called forward at large meetings for public recognition and then called to the microphone for impromptu speeches. That may be the opposite of a reward for an introvert; a boss needs to think not about the Golden Rule (treat others as you want to be treated) but the Platinum Rule[2] (treat others as *they* would like to be treated).

If you are an introvert with an extroverted boss, the same one-sentence advice that applied above applies here: negotiate! Let your boss know what you need from him. At the same time, when you know that your boss is going to say, "Hey, how's it going?" be prepared! The politically correct response is more than just a grunt. Every once in a while, be prepared for a five-minute chat. Even better, think about how you can get to know your boss's interests and ask her a few questions; that is an easy way for an introvert to engage in conversation ("How was your golf game Saturday, boss?").

HOW TO BE MORE BALANCED IF YOU'RE AN EXTROVERT

The number-one way for an extrovert to be more balanced is to stop talking! And stop for more than a few seconds. Ten seconds is not a long time, but it will seem like forever. If you're talking to an introvert and it is his turn to talk, stop talking and count to 10 in your head.

Number two: Ask questions. And make sure they can't be

answered with a simple yes or no. Ask open-ended questions—don't say, "Do you agree?" Say, "What do you think?" or "What are your thoughts on this?"

Take your cues from other people, and understand whom you are dealing with. An introvert will tend to answer questions slowly and without a lot of detail. You need to ask open-ended questions and be patient with silence.

For the extroverted co-worker, all of the above applies. In addition, if you have a lot of introverted co-workers, you may need to remember that people are not trying to hurt your feelings when they don't join you for coffee breaks or invite you to lunch. You may need to look outside your immediate work group for coffee-break conversations or lunch-group friends.

For the extroverted boss, know your employees. A simple "How is everybody?" will not do for an introvert. Nor will a general question thrown out in the meeting. Use the technique mentioned above, where the agenda is distributed ahead of time.

For the extroverted employee, especially one with an introverted boss, just remember that you won't always know what your boss is thinking. You need to remember to ask. You also need to remember not to assume. It is easy to assume the worst with the introverted boss. Ask questions, and keep asking. But remember to stop talking after you ask.

HOW TO BE MORE BALANCED IF YOU'RE AN INTROVERT

Script your speeches ahead of time. This works for social small talk, for meetings, or for any other time that you're going to be faced with having to begin conversations. This would have worked for Marco and Janet in our earlier case study. In addition to doing the research about who was attending the conference, they could have scripted some opening small talk and prepared to talk to the people at the conference.

Introverts need to get meeting agendas ahead of time. They can plan their contributions and know what they're going to say. They need to get the floor before they speak. Get the floor physically by moving forward in the chair, making eye contact around the table, and saying things like, "Well, that's a good point, and here's what I have to say about that," before making the point.

If you are an introverted co-worker, you need to take your cue from other people and understand whom you are dealing with. If you are dealing with a lot of extroverts, know that you are going to have to get out of your comfort zone from time to time. You're going to have to accept invitations to coffee breaks, lunch, and business dinners. Do your homework on the backgrounds of these people, their interests, etc. Plan some ice-breaking small talk ahead of time, ask questions about their current work projects, etc. Watch what extroverts do; there isn't anything magic about it. You can do it too.

For an introverted boss, get out there with your people. Listen to what they talk about. Listen to the Friday chitchat around the water cooler. On Monday morning, ask them about the things they were talking about on Friday. "Pamela, how did you and your husband enjoy the play on Sunday?" "George, did you get your boat out this Saturday?" "How did the bowling tournament go, Maria?"

And if you are an introverted employee, know that you may be a puzzle to your boss. You may need to make an extra effort to speak out when she speaks to you. When she asks, "How was your weekend?" plan to say more than just "fine." When she says, "How is the project going?" the same rule applies. As is true of most introverts, you may have to think about these conversations ahead of time and plan what you're going to say. But you know these conversations are coming, so do plan them so that you can carry your end of them accordingly.

 ## WHAT WE'VE LEARNED ON OUR TRIP TO THE SUN

Extrovert

Positive Characteristics. Extroverts are outgoing, sociable, and active. They tend to be fun to be around. They have a lot of energy and are talkative and gregarious. Their lights shine brightly.

Negative Characteristics. Because extroverts tend to say what's on their minds, they sometimes lack a filter between the brain and the mouth. So they say things that they sometimes wish they hadn't said. Sometimes they're having so much fun being sociable that the work takes a little longer to get done. They may be easily distracted.

What You Will Get from Them

- No doubt as to what's on their minds

- Lots of feedback

- Lots of opinions

What You Need to Give Them

- A team

- Input from others

- A workplace with a lot of activity

Introvert

Positive Characteristics. Introverts are self-sufficient, quiet, independent, and somewhat reserved. They can work diligently and steadily on a task. They concentrate well.

Negative Characteristics. You may not know what introverts are thinking. They can frustrate a team by seeming to not contribute. They may be seen as aloof or uninterested because they keep their enthusiasm to themselves. They stay out of the light and in the shadows.

What You Will Get from Them

- Focused and diligent work

- A ready ear (good listeners)

- A good facilitator of meetings (can elicit ideas from others)

What You Need to Give Them

- Time alone

- Advance notice of conversations, meeting agendas, questions, etc.

- Open-ended questions

- Silence within which to think about their answers to those questions

AFTER OUR TRIP TO THE SUN

This worksheet will help you think about the concepts presented in this chapter.

1. Which end of the spectrum most characterizes me?

Life of the Party ←――――――――――→ **The Quiet One**

2. How does this trait help me contribute positively to situations?

3. When do I need to "stretch" a bit in the opposite direction?

4. Which end of the spectrum most characterizes those closest to me at work?

(**Note:** You may want to choose to analyze particular co-workers, peers, bosses and/or employees who are particularly problematic for you. You can start that process here and continue it with each chapter. Fill out the sections below for as many "problematic people" as you like and then continue to analyze that person or persons in subsequent chapters.)

MY BOSS

Life of the Party ←――――――――――→ **The Quiet One**

MY CO-WORKERS

Life of the Party ⟵⟶ **The Quiet One**

MY PEERS

Life of the Party ⟵⟶ **The Quiet One**

MY EMPLOYEES

Life of the Party ⟵⟶ **The Quiet One**

5. How can I best call on these people when I need to use their natural abilities?

6. How can I avoid expecting them to do things that fly in the face of their natural style? How can I stop being disappointed in them or angry at them when they do what just comes naturally to them?

7. How can I change my behavior to get along better with these people?

CHAPTER 2
Mercurial Messengers

Mercury was the ancient Roman messenger god. He is often pictured in a pair of winged sandals with which he was reported to be able to move faster than the wind. Mercury is the closest planet to the sun and orbits it once every 88 days, which is the fastest orbit of all of the planets. The Romans reportedly named it after the god Mercury because of its rapid movement in the sky. I'll use this image to talk about a characteristic that describes a person who has a lot of energy and who is very active. Sounds good so far, doesn't it? And it is, until that person comes up against his opposite in the workplace: the person who prefers to think things over, take his time, and work much more slowly.

REFLECTORS/ACTORS

Reflectors are *relaxed* and like to *take their time*. Actors are *tense*, *action-oriented*, and have a *sense of urgency* about them. As with all of the traits, these two can be complementary, allowing both types to work together effectively. However, it is essential for each to understand where the other is coming from and specify expectations at the outset so that misunderstandings don't occur.

For example, your colleague in the next cubicle might say to you one day, "Let's get together and brainstorm about the Simpson project." "Great idea!" you reply. Then you forget all about it. To you, the conversation meant, "Someday we ought to do that." To your peer, it meant you should set up a time to go to the nearest conference room together, preferably today or tomorrow.

BEFORE WE TRAVEL TO MERCURY

A number of personality-research studies have discovered this difference between reflecting and acting. Several psychological tests measure things like how oriented we are toward taking action, our sense of urgency, the amount of thought and data we desire before we reach a decision, and our activity level. In psychological language, extreme ends of the spectrum of the reflective/active characteristic would be described as depressed and manic. (And of course, one person can swing back and forth if he suffers from bipolar disorder or manic depression.) I am talking here about the "normal" portion of the continuum between action and reflection.

Which End of the Spectrum Most Characterizes Me?

Do you like to keep busy? Does sitting at a desk all day drive you crazy? Do you make decisions quickly, do you like to take action, and do you get impatient with a lot of talk about issues? Or are you just the opposite? Does it make you nervous when people act too quickly? Are you the one who wants to collect more data and think it over a little more? Do you find it restful to sit at your desk and reflect on the issues a bit before leaping into action? Does a lot of activity make you tired?

Which End of the Spectrum Most Characterizes Those Closest to Me at Work: My Boss, My Co-Workers, My Peers, and My Employees?

Do you see either or both of these types around you at work? Are there those who are always active, make decisions quickly, and come across in a very energetic fashion? And are there others who seem much more reflective, want to think things over, and come across as having much less energy?

MERCURIAL PARTNERS

Jake and Ben are in their mid-20s and have recently begun a partnership in a new financial-planning business. They became friends in college, and after several years of working for various financial institutions, they decided to strike out on their own. For the past several months, they have been setting up office space and planning their business venture while winding down their current responsibilities at their individual jobs.

One day, Jake pulled his car up to a line of cars waiting at the curbside-unloading zone at the airport. "It's crowded today," he said to Ben. "I hope we left you enough time. Have a great time at the wedding, and remember to tell your sister congratulations for me. I'll pick you up right here—a week from today, right? Be sure to e-mail me your flight number."

"This line sure isn't moving very fast," commented Ben. "Anyway, we'll have this week to think about what we want to do once I get back. We've got a lot of work to do on the office. Let's think about what we want to do on updating the computer system, for one thing. I'm also thinking we're at the point where we could hire an assistant, a sort of an office manager/administrative person. And we could just overhaul the setup of the whole place. I feel sometimes like I'm working out of a garage or a warehouse. You know what I mean?"

"Oh yeah," said Jake. "It's okay for a start-up, but we're going to start seeing clients in there and we already need to update what we are doing. All right, our line is moving now. Get going, buddy—got your suitcase? Have a great trip."

One week later, Jake picks Ben up at the airport. "Let's stop off at the office before I take you home," said Jake. "I can't wait to show you what I've done."

"Wait a minute," said Ben. "What you've done? I thought we were going to get together and plan it once I got back?"

A half-hour later, Ben was looking around him in shock. The

office had been painted, new furniture had been brought in, a stranger was smiling at him from behind a new desk, and new computer equipment was in evidence. Then he turned to his partner and pulled some papers out of his briefcase. "Well, here's an article I pulled out of the in-flight magazine on the best computer equipment for our kind of business, and here's some diagrams I made on the flight back on some ideas on the best office furniture setup for a business like ours, and here are some references I got for office managers and administrators, but I guess you don't want to see those." He threw the papers in the air and walked out of the office.

"Thanks a lot!" said Jake, furious. "Here I do all this work while you take it easy for a week, and this is the thanks I get?"

What we have here is a failure to communicate, on a big level! Can these two be partners? Both expected praise and recognition for their work over the past week. Ben had thought, reflected, and ruminated. Jake took action. Both had simply followed their natural instincts. Now each is thoroughly angry with the other.

MERCURY AT REST: CHARACTERISTICS OF REFLECTORS

Reflectors prefer to relax and think, which makes the best use of their limited physical energies. They make good delegators. They need time to think during the work day; a busy day with every moment scheduled does not make the most effective use of their time. Reflectors tend to be reliable, balanced, and idea-oriented. They like to plan more than they like to act.

Reflectors like to deal with the abstract more than the concrete. They are intuitive, perceptive, relaxed, and somewhat cautious, meaning that they don't like to take a lot of risks or move very quickly when making a decision. They can, however, be creative once they have gathered enough data to be comfortable making a decision. Reflectors take a while making decisions because they like to consider all sides of the issue and do not like to feel rushed. They like to consider all of the long-term implications.

MERCURY RISING: CHARACTERISTICS OF ACTORS

Actors are at their best when on the move all day long. They enjoy, and can handle, constant activity. They are active and generally appear to be in a good mood (although subject to "moodiness" sometimes). They often appear energetic and give off an air of excitement. People who have this high energy, especially if they are also extroverted (see chapter 1), may be quite talkative.

Actors are task-oriented and like to get things organized. They want and need to stay physically active. They tend to work quickly and make quick decisions. Their high energy level and desire for activity makes them very hands-on in their approach to work. This means that many of them do not like to delegate, and this can cause problems when actors are managers.

Actors make decisions quickly and in a logical fashion. They tend to assess rapidly what data is needed to make a decision, gather it quickly, and move forward. There is no implication here that they make decisions in a sloppy or impulsive fashion, although the reflectors tend to misperceive them as doing so.

MERCURIAL COMBINATIONS

What happens when two reflectors get together, or two actors, or one of each?

Two Reflectors

When two reflectors get together, there is little conflict between them. They relax, they plan, and they gather data. Then they may go back and gather more data. The conflict occurs when their boss comes to them to get the report or the project only to find that they have hardly started. The reflectors are chagrined that the boss even expected them to have a finished product ready. "How can you expect us to be done already?" they ask. "There is no way we could do that report in only one day. We will have it to you by the end of the week. Maybe." They are simply not comfortable making decisions quickly, nor are they action-oriented. They are very comfortable reflecting on all the possibilities and are not prompted by the pressures of a deadline. Instead, they may feel that the deadline is arbitrary and unreasonable.

Their limited physical energy is also very real. When they need to take a break or get something to eat or drink, this may be seen as a weakness by the more energetic co-worker, who can go on and on without taking a break. The reflector, on the other hand, works much more effectively if allowed reasonable breaks.

Two Actors

When two actors get together, they may get along just fine also. Their workplace will be a whirlwind of activity and excitement. They will work quickly, take time to go out for a good lunch, have some fun, and get the project done. The lunch, by the way, is not taken to get a break from the activity but possibly to get even more activity into the day. They will not go to a quiet out-of-the-way spot for lunch; they'll go somewhere very active, perhaps a sports bar.

Two or more actors on the team will have a report or project on their boss's desk on time, or perhaps even prior to the deadline, and the report may be done quite well—or not—depending on many other factors, such as their conscientiousness perhaps. But they will do it quickly because their decisions are made quickly, and they will gather data quickly.

Sometimes, because of this quickness and impulsivity, the project or task is a bit rough around the edges. There are many other factors, as I mentioned, that affect the quality of the task, but all other things being equal, a team full of actors who are extremely activity-oriented may tend to miss some of the data and detail simply because they are moving so quickly.

One of Each

If a reflector and an actor are working together, each will make the other very nervous. A reflector may see an actor as restless, impatient, simplistic, staying busy just for the sake of being busy, and impulsive in her decision making. An actor may charge a reflector with being lazy or indecisive. The reflector may become exhausted working with a group of actors. And an actor will become frustrated and impatient sitting around with a group of reflectors. Let's look at some examples of the various ways this relationship could play out.

Co-Workers. The actor will gather her data quickly and assess it quickly. The reflector will see this as a waste of energy and feel that the actor should slow down. "What's your rush?" the reflector might ask. "The project isn't due until next Friday anyway." Besides, the reflector is probably already thinking about other sources of information that might be available and may be wondering if the actor could have gotten nearly enough information in the time she spent. The actor, in turn, will see this additional data gathering as unnecessary and a waste of time. When it comes to decision making, accusations will fly; the actor will accuse the reflector of being a foot dragger, and the reflector will accuse the actor of shooting from the hip.

Like Jake and Ben in our opening case study, a reflector and an actor who work together must be sure to communicate very clearly. Nothing should be left to assumption. They almost work together best if they work sequentially; the reflector does the prework, gathers the data, and does the planning, and the actor implements the project. Their expectations of each other need to be very clear. An actor can't expect the reflector to keep up with her in terms of energy expenditure. A reflector simply doesn't expend energy the same way an actor does. A reflector isn't on the go eight or 10 (or 12) hours a day; in fact, a reflector would be exhausted by that pace. And the reflector can't expect an actor to sit down, relax, and ruminate over the various issues at hand. An actor would put up with that for about five minutes.

So, can Jake and Ben be partners? With an understanding of each other's style, they can be. If they continue to misunderstand, they are going to fail miserably. Like most of the traits I've been talking about, opposite styles need each other. If they were both alike, if they were both actors or both reflectors, they would have a much more difficult time establishing a successful business. If they recognize and appreciate the fact that they have two complementary styles, they can build on each other's strengths, support each other's weaknesses, and utilize what each does best to build their organization.

How can they do that? They can do that by simply assessing what needs to be done, when it needs to be done, and who the appropriate person is to do it. When quick decisions and quick deadlines are looming, Jake is the one to step in and take over. It seems that in this case, Ben will be more effective behind the scenes. He can be the planner, the researcher, and the one who will be more effective when he can take his time. Because their's is a financial-planning business, perhaps they will decide that Jake will be the client handler and Ben will be the office administrator and paperwork handler.

Boss and Employee. If the boss is the reflector, he is going to have to be a particularly good communicator to deal with staff members who are actors. The staff is not going to take his most offhand comments lightly. If he says, "We ought to think about doing X," he should not be surprised if, when he comes to work the next day, it is already done. Perhaps he meant they should think about it. Perhaps he wanted to do some research first, or maybe he meant that it should be done a different way. That is what he needs to communicate immediately, and set expectations for, rather than make offhand comments that his actors may well act on.

He also needs to think about how to channel this activity in a way that best benefits his department. Although the reflector boss may find all of these actor employees exhausting, their energy can actually be of great value to him. This is energy, remember, that he doesn't have. And he is a good delegator. So he needs to get over his nervousness about acting too quickly sometimes, and when things need to get done, send his actor employees out to get it done. They will enjoy the activity much more than he ever will, they will find some opportunities to develop their skills, and the boss will get a much-needed break.

Employee and Boss. When the boss is an actor who manages reflectors, there are a couple of issues to consider. First of all, the actor boss doesn't particularly like to delegate. After all, he is an actor. He is busy all the time, he likes to stay active, and he has a high energy level. He's too busy doing things to delegate his tasks to others. This means he's doing a disservice to his employees. They don't learn, they don't grow, and they aren't empowered to do the tasks they need to do. He also tends to misunderstand his staff members because they have lower energy levels than he does. In fact, their energy levels may be more normal than his is, but he sees lower energy as a sign of uncaring, laziness, or a lack of urgency.

The second problem with the boss as an actor is that he doesn't benefit from the thinking or reflection that's going on among his staff. They may be gathering data that could probably benefit him in the long run. He needs to find a way to tap into this. I will talk about this more in the next sections on how to be more balanced.

HOW TO BE MORE BALANCED IF YOU'RE A REFLECTOR

If you are a reflector who needs to work with actors, you are probably well aware of the frustrations that can ensue. You're exhausted by the constant activity around you. You're the only one who feels like going on a break at the regularly scheduled break times. You feel rushed quite a bit of the time. You feel pushed into decisions that you are not ready to make. You have to turn over projects that you don't feel are ready or finished. You may feel that it's ridiculous to be working so hard on a project that isn't due until some time in the future. You feel robbed of quiet reflection time that would make a decision, a task, or a project go more smoothly or be of higher quality if you were allowed your planning time. You are astonished when, at quitting time, when you are ready to go home, the actors all say, "Let's grab the conference room now that it's empty and prepare the agenda for next week's meeting."

So what is a reflector to do? A preemptive strike is best. Find out ahead of time what the decision or project is going to be. Do your planning and reflecting prior to the meeting when you know the decision is going to be discussed. Don't proudly display all of the data that you have collected for your actor co-workers; remember, they don't need all of that data, you do. Jump into the discussion in a way that fits in better with their style and you'll come across as a better teammate. You will have eased your frustration by doing the prework, and you will ease their frustration with you by acting, in the meeting, more in line with the group norm.

When it's quitting time or break time, don't make a big deal of it. But take the time that you need to maintain your energy. Don't do it every time, but sometimes do go along with them, and spend the extra time. Work over your break and stay with the team if it is preparing a report past quitting time. Other times, don't just say, "No, it's quitting time, and I'm going home," or "No, I'm going on a break even if no one else is." Say something a bit more actor-friendly like, "Oh, I'd love to stay and I'm sorry I'll miss the meeting, but I've got an important appointment this evening that I can't miss. Be sure to fill me in tomorrow on what you all decide." That way you preserve your energy and preserve your standing in the group as well. Just don't overuse this technique.

A reflector boss must remember two things when dealing with actors, whether they are your employees, your peers, or others in the organization. The first is similar to the advice I gave to the co-workers: Do the reflective work preemptively, not in meetings or in the presence of actors who will be frustrated and annoyed by it. Second, and this is particularly important in the presence of your employees, it is critical that you be a clear communicator. Your employees will take your every offhand comment as a call to action. Instead of saying, "We ought to think about straightening up this office," you need to say something like, "Monday at our staff meeting I'm going to include an agenda item on remodeling the office. Come prepared with ideas that we will reach agreement on regarding new equipment, new furniture, new paint, and new blinds." And remember to preserve your energy when you need to, but do so in a tactful and diplomatic fashion.

What if you are an employee who is a reflector, and you have an actor boss? There are some special implications here. Your boss is very likely to misunderstand your style, think that you have low energy, perhaps even that you are uncaring, and that you have no sense of urgency about tasks or projects. Once again, in this case communication can be key. You need to let your boss know what is going on behind the scenes.

First of all, communicate the value of the data that you are collecting and the energy that you are expending in your own way on projects and tasks. Second, push yourself to show a little bit more energy, the way that actors do, so that your boss does not misunderstand. Work through your break if the rest of the work group is doing so. Don't leave work right at five o'clock if no one else seems to be doing so. If you find yourself in a constant state of exhaustion, you may be in the wrong organization. You may simply be in an organization full of extreme actors— dare we say a "manic" organization—and you may not be a good fit there. If you remain in this state of exhaustion, you may have to decide whether the organization is the best fit for you and you may want to look for a different job.

Or perhaps you simply have to go outside of your comfort zone a bit, make decisions faster, and do projects in a way that makes you slightly uncomfortable. No, you don't have all of the data and you don't have the time to reflect on it that you wish you had, but the boss is the boss and the deadline is the deadline. The first couple of times you do this may feel a bit uncomfortable to you, but when you realize that the project or task was in fact quite satisfactory to your boss, you may begin to become more balanced and realize that a little bit of a push and a little bit more activity really aren't such bad things.

HOW TO BE MORE BALANCED IF YOU'RE AN ACTOR

If you are an actor and you have reflecting co-workers, I know you're frustrated by them also. But you can learn from them as well. Sometimes a little more data does help in the decision-making process. Sometimes a project does improve with a little more time spent in discussion. Sometimes the fastest way isn't the best way. Try this: If you have 30 minutes to spare at your next meeting, sit back in your chair and ask everyone around the table for any additional thoughts on the decision at hand. I know what you're thinking, what a waste of time, right? But it is an interesting process and is something that reflectors do quite frequently. And it can bring up some new and valuable data that you may not have thought about otherwise.

Your reflector co-workers simply don't have the same energy level that you do. They really are going to work more effectively when they come back from that break they insist on taking. Let them take it. And don't do their work for them while they're gone. It wouldn't hurt you to take a break with them once in a while. Perhaps you could chat over coffee and learn some things that way.

What about the boss who is an actor? As I said earlier, the issue with the actor boss is that she likes to keep so busy that delegating can be an issue. This is a problem for the development of her staff. For an actor boss to become more balanced, she really needs to learn how to take some pride in the accomplishments of other people. After all, the basic definition of management is getting things done through other people. An actor boss typically will benefit from course work in things like coaching and delegating.

The second issue here is what to do with all of those reflectors who may be on her staff. An actor boss must remind herself that these people are not slackers, and they are not sitting around at their desks napping. Their reflection time and their data gathering can actually be of some value to the organization, to the task at hand, and to the project. In this scenario as well, communication can be key. The boss needs to tap into these reflectors and utilize their data, yet set realistic deadlines and see that they are followed.

The other issue for the actor boss to consider is that the reflector employee simply has a naturally lower energy level. This does not mean that this person's sense of urgency is any less, that he is uncaring, or that he is a lazy. There are many other factors that go into quality of work, such as conscientiousness, detail-orientation, etc. It is critical that a boss look below the surface of a reflector employee and not make snap judgments based on energy level.

As an actor employee, what if you find yourself with a reflector boss? This can be a frustrating situation as well, but once again, the boss is still the boss. You want to keep busy, in fact, you need to keep busy. This can actually be of great value to your boss, except that you might drive him crazy. The problem occurs when your boss delegates the data gathering to you, which is something that you're not very good at. Negotiation is the key here. Let your boss know what your strengths are, and take on all the "quick activity" work from him that you can.

Enter into the reflections and data gathering, when possible, and curb your frustration with it as much as you can, but volunteer for everything that you know will be a frustration to your boss: quick activities, tasks with fast-approaching deadlines, etc. You will establish your value quickly in that fashion.

 ## WHAT WE'VE LEARNED ON OUR TRIP TO MERCURY

Reflector

Positive Characteristics. Reflectors often show good judgment and good common sense. They tend to be adaptable, think clearly, and are reasonable. Because they like to collect a lot of data, they often have the pros and cons of any argument or decision close at hand.

Negative Characteristics. Reflectors generally tend to have lower energy levels. This may cause them to look apathetic or uncaring about the task at hand. Actors may accuse them of not having a sense of urgency.

What You Will Get from Them

- Planning
- Caution
- Low energy level

What You Need to Give Them

- Ability to make unhurried decisions (time)
- Freedom from constant activity (allow for break times)
- Teammates or assistants they can delegate to

Actor

Positive Characteristics. Actors are energetic, open, and enthusiastic. They tend to have a curiosity about life in general, are generally pleasant to be around, have a self-confident air, and have a certain amount of ambition.

Negative Characteristics. Actors can be too impulsive. They may not take the time to consider the ramifications of their actions. Although reflectors sometimes falsely accuse them of making decisions too quickly, the accusations are sometimes true.

What You Will Get from Them

- Action
- Quick decisions
- Energy

What You Need to Give Them

- Opportunity for physical activity
- Challenging tasks
- Freedom from lengthy data gathering

AFTER OUR TRIP TO MERCURY

This worksheet will help you think about the concepts presented in this chapter.

1. Which end of the spectrum most characterizes me?

Reflector ← → Actor

2. How does this trait help me contribute positively to situations?

3. When do I need to "stretch" a bit in the opposite direction?

4. Which end of the spectrum most characterizes those closest to me at work? (If you have chosen to analyze your boss,

particular co-workers, and/or employees who are particularly problematic for you, continue to analyze that person or persons here.)

MY BOSS

Reflector — Actor

MY CO-WORKERS

Reflector — Actor

MY PEERS

Reflector — Actor

MY EMPLOYEES

Reflector — Actor

5. How can I best call on these people when I need to use their natural abilities?

6. How can I avoid expecting them to do things that fly in the face of their natural style? How can I stop being disappointed in them or angry at them when they do what just comes naturally to them?

7. How can I change my behavior to get along better with these people?

CHAPTER 3
Venusians in the Workplace

Ancient astronomers thought that the planet Venus was two different bodies; they referred to it as both "the morning star" and "the evening star." Venus is named after the ancient Roman goddess of love. It is considered the most beautiful of the planets and has come to be connected with love and other sensitive emotions. The characteristic I am going to relate to the planet Venus has to do with sensitivity and emotion and how we use those traits in our decision-making processes.

LOGICAL/SENSITIVE

Have you ever felt like you were getting nowhere in resolving a difference of opinion because the other person in the dispute was coming from an entirely different place? For example, perhaps you presented all of the logical reasons your work group should pursue a particular project and your co-worker countered with all of the emotional reasons why you should not.

The sensitive person is *emotional, insightful,* and *socially perceptive*. The logical person is more *literal, factual,* and *tough-*

minded. Each gathers data from entirely different places when faced with a decision-making situation. Both types of data are important in making the decision, but it is critical to understand why you may not be getting anywhere in resolving a difference of opinion.

BEFORE WE TRAVEL TO VENUS

The Jungian temperament research, which I talked about in the introduction, described the difference between thinkers and feelers. Thinkers like to rely on the facts in order to make a decision, and feelers prefer to factor in things like what people value and what they are feeling. In Chapter 5, I will talk about concrete thinkers versus intuitive thinkers and how people like to obtain information prior to making a decision. In this chapter, when I talk about thinking and feeling, I am referring to how people like to make their decisions and on what they feel decisions should be based.

Thinking and *feeling* are the words used to describe the very divergent ways people come to conclusions about things or make decisions. Thinking and feeling refer to different ways of processing the data that flows into our heads; thinkers, or the people I will refer to as "logical," prefer to be objective and factual, but feelers, whom I will call "sensitive," are more subjective and prefer to take personal values into account rather than logic. Obviously, the two can arrive at very different solutions to the same problem because the criteria they use to evaluate it are so different.

Which End of the Spectrum Most Characterizes Me?

Do you tend to make decisions based on logic and the facts at hand, and do you try to stay objective? Do you look at the pros and cons from the outside, as it were? Or do you feel more subjective about issues? Do you base your decision on how you feel and how you think others might feel and be affected by the decision? Are your personal values important in most decision-making processes?

Which End of the Spectrum Most Characterizes Those Closest to Me at Work: My Boss, My Co-Workers, My Peers, and My Employees?

What about those you work closest with? Do they tend to make decisions with charts, graphs, and numbers-based research? Or do they favor customer focus groups and employee opinion surveys? Do they talk in terms of values, feelings, and effects, or numbers, profits, and loss?

VENUSIANS CAN'T AGREE ON WHO BELONGS IN THE ZOO

Linda Hanf has been the new manager at the large call center (affectionately known to the employees as "The Zoo") for a month now. It is open seven days a week from 7 a.m. to 10 p.m., handles calls from customers of a cable television company, and has 300 employees with 12 supervisors. Eight of the supervisors, who have been there for between eight and 10 years, work the day shift Monday through Friday. The four new supervisors work on weekends and evenings.

The problem that Linda has identified is that new employees are also scheduled weekends and evenings. When difficult customer problems arise, the brand-new supervisors and the brand-new employees often struggle to find answers to the problems. It was evident that there was one logical solution to the problem: The seasoned supervisors should be working with the newer employees.

Linda had arranged, not without some difficulty, to get all 12 supervisors to a meeting today. She has planned to present them with a couple of answers to this dilemma and ask for their input as to the correct solution. It had long been a custom at the call center that as new employees became more tenured they were rewarded by moving from night and weekend to day and weekday shifts. Linda was going to suggest changes to the schedule. Either the seasoned employees had to work weekends and evenings, or the seasoned supervisors had to work evenings and weekends, or they had to work out some kind of a rotation.

When she opened the meeting with this presentation, she was met with flat silence. Then Alice Olson, one of the supervisors with 10 years of experience, began to cry. "Absolutely not," she said. "One of the only perks to working here for all these years is that we get to spend evenings and weekends with our families. If you take that away, we have nothing."

It became evident from some of the faces around the table that several of the other supervisors agreed with Alice. "The employees aren't going to go for it either," mentioned one of them. "It has always been well-known that once you've been here a few years, you no longer have to work the weekend and evening shifts."

Linda made an attempt to get back on track. "I appreciate what you're all saying. But none of you have addressed my concerns. A lot of our best customers work during the week, so they are home watching television in the evening or on weekends. When they call with an issue during those times, they get brand-new employees who can't handle their problems, and when the employees call for a supervisor, they get a brand-new supervisor. Is that fair to our customers? Is that fair to our company?"

Silence.

RATIONAL VENUS: CHARACTERISTICS OF LOGICAL PEOPLE

The people I have characterized as "logical" think in terms of schedules and priorities. They use reason and logic in their approach to decision making. They are unlikely to be convinced by anything except reason and logic. The correct answer to a problem is often so evident to them that they go ahead and fix things and then are surprised by people's emotional reaction to their solutions. They don't take things personally themselves, and they don't expect others to do so. They are easily able to step back from a problem and take a cool, impersonal approach to problem solving and decision making.

EMOTIONAL VENUS: CHARACTERISTICS OF SENSITIVE PEOPLE

"Sensitive" people tend to use their values and their subjective judgment when making decisions. They may be guided by the kind of criteria in decision making that leads them to ask questions like, What will allow us to avoid conflict? They are guided by how they feel about the problem and how they think others might feel about it. Their personal values enter into the decision, and they tend to take things personally. It is not only difficult for them to step back and look at a problem coolly and impersonally, it doesn't make sense for them to do so, because problems by their very nature do involve people and do involve values. What sense does it make to try to pretend problems are impersonal?

VENUSIAN COMBINATIONS

So what happens when two logical people work together? Or two sensitive people? Or one of each? Let's take a look.

Two Logical People

Two rational Venusians can reach a decision practically and efficiently. They will rely on the facts, put together as many charts, graphs, and logical arguments as are required, and present the sound, reasonable arguments that led to their decision. They will work together in harmony and will admire each other's ability to think clearly and rationally.

Of course, the downside is that sometimes people's feelings and values do need to be taken into account. Other people in the organization may resist or even completely reject the logic.

Two Sensitive People

Two emotional Venusians will also get along very well when making a decision together. They will speak the same language, consider the feelings and values of the people involved, and come to their decisions based on the same kind of criteria.

Once again, however, the logical people in the organization may resist or reject their decisions and give no credence to their points of view. The logical people may say that the sensitive people paid little or no attention to the logic or rationale of the facts at hand.

One of Each

As we have often seen, one of each can be a match made in heaven or a situation ripe for conflict. Linda and her supervisors in the opening case study are at a stalemate. How can these kinds of situations be resolved? The ideal situation is one in which everyone considers both the facts and the feelings of people when the decision is made. Can this be done? Let's see how it works.

Co-Workers. When a logical person and a sensitive person work together, they each have a common and very serious problem when they try to communicate. When they find themselves getting nowhere in an argument, they simply bring forth more of the material that it takes to convince themselves. That does nothing to convince their partners. Let's look at an example.

Noko and William are on an employee committee to choose a new vendor for their company's cafeteria. They are down to two choices: Universal Foods and Café Services. Noko is in favor of Universal Foods and has drawn up the profit figures showing that it would benefit the company overall to use Universal Foods as its vendor. William worked for another organization in the past that used Universal Foods as a vendor for its cafeteria. He didn't care for their food, and in fact once became ill after eating lunch there. Yes, it's true there was a stomach virus going around the company at the time, but he has a bad feeling about Universal Foods. Under no circumstances does he want to see them come in to his current company and take over the cafeteria offerings.

At this point, rational Noko makes the usual mistake. She begins to try to convince emotional William by using more facts and more logic. She asks him to visit some current cafeterias where Universal Foods does business. She uses scientific measures; she shows him their recent health reports. She shows him that the health department has taken samples of their hot and cold foods and shown that the levels of bacteria are well within healthful standards. William simply shudders.

What Noko does not understand is that William is not objecting to Universal Foods on logical or rational grounds. He is objecting to them on an emotional level, and he will not be swayed on a logical or rational level.

The same would be true, of course, if this situation were reversed. Suppose William was very enthusiastic about Café Services. He loved their food and the ambience of their offerings, and he was fond of their owners. Noko was not so happy with their track record of health inspections and profitability. William, of course, in attempting to talk her over to his side, kept bringing up how nice the owners were, how lovely their brochures looked, what a nice presentation they made with their food, etc. Again, without some work and some thought, both sides in this debate tend to make the same error. They are bringing up data that would convince themselves, not information that would even begin to make inroads into the other person's perspective.

Noko should look for some emotional hooks to convince William of the value of Universal Foods. Perhaps she should arrange a meeting with their owners—not a conventional business meeting, but a friendly, sociable meeting. At that meeting, she could ask the owners to arrange for a sampling of some of their best foods. She could also show William their nicest brochures. Now keep in mind, these things don't enter into Noko's decision-making process at all. But knowing what she knows of William now, she knows that these are the kinds of things that may sway him to her side of the argument.

And William should do just the opposite. Rather than continue to try to sway Noko with emotional arguments, he needs to look into the facts and figures about Café Services. He needs to present Noko with some information about their profitability, their ability to make money for the company, etc. He needs to realize that she doesn't care how nice the owners are or how lovely their brochures look.

Boss and Employee. If you are a logical boss, like Linda in the opening case study, and have sensitive employees, like Alice or William, you have the legitimate power of the organization behind you and can simply dictate policy. But in the case of the call center, at what cost would that kind of dictation come? Long-term supervisors may become extremely unhappy, and a lot of employees would probably quit, depending on what the job market was like.

As I advised in Noko's situation, what the logical boss needs to do is present less logic and reason and more emotion and values to employees. Perhaps Linda could try to bring up some empathy for the customers. She could say, "Imagine you're at home with your husband and your kids on a Saturday night, and your cable goes out. You just ordered a movie. You phone the call center to get your cable turned back on, but it's a complicated problem and you get one of our newer employees. He calls a supervisor, it's a half hour later, now the kids are crying, and it's closer to their bedtime. Your nice evening at home is starting to get more and more stressful."

Linda is getting a little smarter now. Alice and the rest are starting to listen to her because she is speaking their language. And remember, even among the seasoned supervisors, who have a stake in wanting to continue to work weekdays, there are some logical individuals who were listening to her from the beginning.

Linda continues. "I know this is something very new I'm suggesting, and I know it's going to be very difficult on both the supervisors and the employees. So I'm asking for your help. How can we set it up so that it's fair to everyone? Can we set up some kind of a rotation? Think about it, and let's get together again in one week. I want to have this new rotation set up so that we can take care of our customers better, and I'd like to see it implemented no later than a month from now."

So with some preparation, some appreciation expressed for their feelings, some advance notice, and expression in no uncertain terms that this change is going to take place, Linda has a chance to make this happen fairly smoothly. She is also going to have to do some work with the supervisors to put together a communication plan for the employees, which will also have to combine facts and logic with feelings and empathy.

Perhaps the opening gambit will be a memo to all employees (which Linda can follow up on with meetings and other types of communication).

To: All employees
From: Linda Hanf, Call Center Manager
Subject: Schedule Rotations

Thank you all for the welcome you have given me as your new manager this past month. I have managed to meet almost everyone and appreciate the time you have spent with me.

I wanted to share with you one concern I have and ask for your support in making some changes. As you know, we have always had new employees start on the night and weekend shifts, then move to weekdays as they got more time in. I understand that those shifts are more desirable and have been considered a reward for people who have more time in with the organization.

My concern is that with the amount of calls we have coming in at night and on the weekends, it just doesn't make any sense to have the newest employees and newest supervisors working those shifts. Our customers are at home with their families trying to spend pleasant evenings watching the movies they've chosen, and instead they're faced with a lot of stress, anxiety, and extra time getting their problems solved. We're going to figure out a way that we can get those customers' problems solved quickly by having experienced employees and supervisors available evenings and weekends. We're going to do this in a fair way, and on a rotating basis. For example, you may end up working one weekend a month, and you will always have the opportunity to request which weekend you want that to be, in case you have some special family events coming up.

Your supervisors and I are still working out the details, but I wanted to let you know right away what was coming up. We'll have the details of the schedule planned by the end of this month. Please let me or your supervisor know if you have any questions. Thank you.

Employee and Boss. If you are a sensitive boss and have logical employees, your issues are a little bit different but the approach to solving them is fairly similar. Your sensitive and emotional approach to problem solving may be wasted on some of your employees. Your appeals to them may seem to get you nowhere; that is your first clue that you are dealing with logical people. As the boss, of course, you have the ability simply to set policy by any criteria you see fit. But why not take the time to speak the language of the people who work for you? It is usually quite helpful to have them on your side.

When the emotional appeals and the talk of values have failed, do what I suggested William do in the case of Café Services. Manage your employees with facts, figures, logic, and reason. Yes, I know this is not what convinces you and not what enters into your database when you make your decisions. But if you come across an employee who simply goes blank in the face of your emotional appeals, you are talking to a logical individual, and she will respond much better to facts and reason.

HOW TO BE MORE BALANCED IF YOU'RE LOGICAL

Like all of the traits I've talked about so far, if you were simply born a logical person, it is going to be tough to take a step back and remember to be more sensitive when dealing with people of that nature. Try to remember, though, that the Jungian temperament research showed that about 50 percent of the people of this world are more sensitive than logical. So if you are truly an extremely logical individual, it wouldn't hurt to try and temper your true self a little bit in your dealings with other people.

As a co-worker, you can probably tell by now why you work so well with some of the people around you and why you just don't do so well with others. Your fellow logical co-workers jump right into the facts and logic with you, love the charts and graphs you come up with, and use the same data you do to make decisions. But remember, that's only about half of the people whom you're liable to come across. When you find yourself in a stalemate, sit back and listen. Are people talking about how they feel, how this affects them personally, and what they value? Recognize that, tell them that you understand, and if you can, tell them how you feel about it. If you're trying to convince them to see things your way, stop giving them more facts and see if you can come up with emotional or feeling arguments. Really think about how you feel about something, and tell them that, not just what you think about it.

As a boss, you need to think about and assess the people you have working for you. Depending upon the company, the industry, or the area of specialization, you may have more logical people or more sensitive people in your department. I don't want to make any generalizations or advance any stereotypes, but one might speculate that, for example, computer programmers or accountants might tend to be more logical, but social workers or teachers might tend to be more sensitive. At any rate, a logical manager needs to assess and be familiar with those who work for him. As I said earlier, one can always set policy arbitrarily, but why not work with people instead and get them on your side? To be more balanced, a logical manager needs to get used to thinking in terms of feelings, values, and emotions. This will be a foreign language at first, but when the manager sees the results this gets with his sensitive employees, this "feeling" language will become easier to speak.

In the case of the logical employee who has a sensitive boss, some of the same issues apply. In an attempt to make inroads with his boss, the logical employee will continue to take facts, figures, charts, and graphs to his boss to make his point. Much to his frustration, the employee gets nowhere. If the boss is a sensitive person who tends to think in terms of feelings and values, the employee needs to change his approach. The employee needs to talk in terms of how he feels about the issue at hand. Again, I know this is hard, and the temptation will be to slip into talking about what he thinks. None of this is easy, as I have said all along. We're talking about changing the habits of a lifetime and changing things about ourselves that are essentially inborn traits. But remember, our behavior is under our direct control and can be changed with some time and practice.

IF YOU'RE SENSITIVE

The sensitive person will probably have a tougher time trying to be more logical than the logical person does trying to be more sensitive. But again, remember that half the world out there is looking at things differently than you are. It's going to make it easier to get things done at work if you can be a little more balanced.

As a co-worker, when you find yourself getting nowhere when it's decision-making or problem-solving time, take a quick assessment of the people with whom you're working. Are they those annoying logical types? You may need to tone down the emotional, feeling-based appeals that you are making. What do you think about the problem? What are the facts? You may need to look carefully at their charts and graphs and make every effort to take in some of the rationale as they are presenting it. Of course, once you have done so, you can always ask them to return the favor by then hearing you out on your opinion on how people are going to respond emotionally to the issue.

As a sensitive boss, just like the logical boss, perhaps your most important job is assessment. What kind of company do you work for? What kind of industry do you work in, what kind of specialists do you have working for you? Who makes up the bulk of your employees: logical or sensitive people? Of course, even if you have the luxury of having sensitive people as the bulk of your employees, chances are you have at least some logical ones mixed in there. And if you are an extremely sensitive individual, it may pay to be a little bit more balanced in all areas of your life. So when you find yourself in a situation where you're clearly dealing with a logical individual and getting nowhere, do your best to speak that person's language. Talk about what you think, not how you feel. Don't ask her how she feels, ask her what she thinks. Enter into a discussion of the facts without bringing up the emotional appeals. And as I said earlier, once you have done this, you may have set the stage for a turn of the tables; in other words, you can then request that she return the favor and allow for a discussion of the sensitive issues that pertain to this situation.

As a sensitive employee working for a logical boss, you may have felt very frustrated in the past. In this situation an employee often feels that his boss is cold, uncaring, aloof, and almost inhuman. I hope this chapter has led you to a clearer understanding that this boss simply has a different way of approaching life and decision making than you have. When you approach this boss, he really doesn't understand the language of how you feel, what you value, etc. You may stand a much better chance getting through to him if you approach him with facts, logic, and reason. For example, you may have asked him for a day off and been turned down. You asked by telling him how you felt about it and asked with an emotional appeal. You would have been better served had you come to him with a simple, factual, logical reason for the day off. The emotional appeal might even have made him uncomfortable, and he turned you down to avoid further conversation about it. To be better balanced in the future, practice talking about what you think about an issue, marshaling the facts about the issue, and avoiding feeling terms, emotional terms, and other such language with a sensitive impact.

 ## WHAT WE'VE LEARNED ON OUR TRIP TO VENUS

Logical

Positive Characteristics. Logical people are objective, and they like to base their decisions on rational logic and thought. They also like to base decisions on standard operating procedures. They think decisions should be fair and just, not made capriciously on what they would consider emotional grounds. They are interested in the reasoning behind decisions.

Negative Characteristics. To those who are more sensitive, logical people may come across as being a bit coldhearted or inhuman. They may see themselves as cool, reserved, and independent, but may come across as aloof and uncaring. They see flaws in logic and point them out, so they may be seen as nitpickers by those who are more sensitive.

What You Will Get from Them

- Justice
- Truth
- Logic
- Fair treatment

What You Need to Give Them

- Respect
- Objectivity
- The facts

Positive Characteristics. Sensitive people make decisions based on their subjective feelings about things. They value affiliation with other people and harmony in relationships. They give appreciation and encouragement to other people.

Negative Characteristics. To the logical people, sensitive people can seem overly softhearted and illogical. They may seem to take things personally and get their feelings hurt too easily. Because they value harmony, they may avoid conflict.

What You Will Get from Them

- Support

- Encouragement

- Mercy

What You Need to Give Them

- Compassion

- A harmonious environment

- A decision-making process that takes values into consideration

AFTER OUR TRIP TO VENUS

This worksheet will help you think about the concepts presented in this chapter.

1. Which end of the spectrum most characterizes me?

Logical ←————————————————————→ **Sensitive**

2. How does this trait help me contribute positively to situations?

3. When do I need to "stretch" a bit in the opposite direction?

4. Which end of the spectrum most characterizes those closest to me at work? (If you have chosen to analyze your boss, particular co-workers, and/or employees who are particularly problematic for you at work, continue to analyze that person or persons here.)

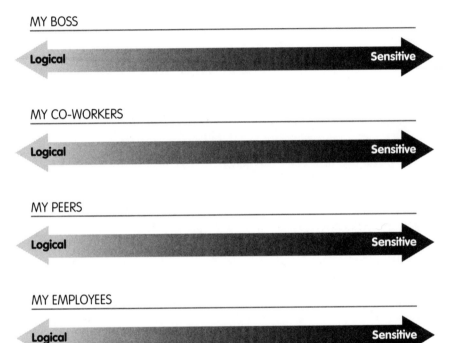

MY BOSS

Logical ——————————————————— Sensitive

MY CO-WORKERS

Logical ——————————————————— Sensitive

MY PEERS

Logical ——————————————————— Sensitive

MY EMPLOYEES

Logical ——————————————————— Sensitive

5. How can I best call on these people when I need to use their natural abilities?

6. How can I avoid expecting them to do things that fly in the face of their natural style? How can I stop being disappointed in them or angry at them when they do what just comes naturally to them?

7. How can I change my behavior to get along better with these people?

CHAPTER 4
Down to Earth

Our planet! Earth—the third rock from the sun. You think you know it so well, but there are so many different places and things to see right here on your home planet. It's not likely that you will visit them all in a single lifetime. You might figure you're on safe ground when you are dealing with your fellow Earthlings. But they come in all kinds of varieties; sometimes you may not even recognize your planetmates. Well, they may not recognize you either.

CARRIED AWAY/FEET ON THE GROUND

This chapter deals with how emotionally controlled people are. The trait I will discuss concerns *not* how emotional people are, but how much they are in control of their emotions versus how much they feel controlled by them. People who have their feet on the ground ("down to earth") are *controlled, calm, poised,* and have the *ability to control their impulses*. People who get carried away ("head in the clouds") tend to *have wider swings* in their emotions. They are *moody, tense,* and *anxious,* and whatever the situation—good or bad—they seem to be more *depressed*, more *elated*, or *more worried* than the situation seems to call for.

BEFORE WE TRAVEL TO THE EARTH

This trait is related to Daniel Goleman's research on emotional intelligence. He talks about impulse control and being "passion's slave"; the goal of learning to be more emotionally intelligent, in his language, is to feel emotions that are more appropriate and more in proportion to the circumstances.

The trait I am talking about in this chapter also has a great deal to do with the "Big Five" characteristic of *emotional stability* that I discussed in the introduction. (It used to be called "neuroticism," but that has a bit of a negative connotation, so researchers have begun calling it emotional stability instead.) Like many of the traits I am discussing, there is a lot of evidence that we bring our personalities to the workplace with us because these traits are inborn. In other words, we have been this way practically since the day we were born. The chances of us changing completely or even a whole lot once we become adults are not great. And the chances of us changing the people around us are even smaller. With some work and some concentration we can make small changes to help us be more balanced, and that is what this book is all about. Keep in mind (and those of you who have small children can probably verify this) that these personality traits began to show themselves at a very early age, so I am talking about the habits of a lifetime. That is why I say that it takes a lot of work and a lot of concentration to change them. But I think I can convince you that, with this trait especially, some small changes may pay off when it comes to your work life and your career.

I have two nieces, Dayna and Erin, who were born within a few months of each other. Dayna seemed very much a "feet on the ground" kind of an individual from the beginning. And Erin, well, Erin got "carried away." When the girls were about four years old or so, their parents took them to an amusement park. When they got off one of the roller coasters, a little boy who got off in front of them did what comes naturally to some kids getting off of a roller coaster—he lost his lunch all over the ground. The sight of the little boy getting sick upset Erin a great deal. And she cried and wailed and kept saying, "That's so gross." Her father tried to soothe her, saying, "But Erin, that's just part of life." Dayna, meanwhile, sat on a nearby bench and placidly ate her ice cream cone, waiting for Erin to come back down to earth and go on the next ride. This was one of the best examples of these two personality types that I had ever seen. And this was in four-year-olds.

Which End of the Spectrum Most Characterizes Me?

Do you tend to take most things in stride? Are you calm most of the time, or would you characterize yourself as nervous and anxious about many things? When faced with a shock, surprising news, a scare, or a sudden crushing disappointment, do you feel out of control and impulsive or reasonably in control?

Which End of the Spectrum Most Characterizes Those Closest to Me at Work: My Boss, My Co-Workers, My Peers, and My Employees?

What about the people you work with most closely? Do you recognize the two ends of the spectrum in your daily life at work? Do you see people who calmly face a crisis even to the point where it makes you wonder if they even "get it"? Do you see other people who create such drama that it makes you tired? I will explore both types in the rest of this chapter.

ON STARSHIP EARTH: STABILITY OR STUPIDITY?

Let's imagine that Ming is one of your employees. She is a bit difficult to deal with. Everything is high drama with her; there are lots of crises, upsets, and traumas in her life. If she experiences a near-miss car accident on the way to work and someone honks a horn at her, she practically has to go home and go back to bed; at best, she worries about it all day. Either way, it almost seems that her day is ruined. Ming is an excellent employee in other ways, though. She has good relationships with her clients and produces good sales numbers consistently.

Joe is also on your sales staff. He is so easy to deal with. He is calm, cool, and collected. He is able to sail through any crisis. And you appreciate that so much after a rough day with Ming.

One day at a staff meeting, you announce that an important piece of video is missing; one that the department was going to use for a presentation to senior staff in the morning. Your company has recently been acquired by another (the whole acquisition process was very rough on Ming, of course), and this is your first chance to show the new owners what you are all about. The video had been prepared especially for this presentation and you have been searching for it all morning. There is only one copy, and you ask for the staff's help in locating it.

Ming might say, "Oh, my gosh! The presentation just won't work without that video, and we sure don't have time to remake it. Let's just start at one end of the department and look in every possible place it could be—tear the place apart. And who has been here in the past couple of days who might have walked off with it? When was the last time anyone saw it?"

Joe might say, "Well, if worst comes to worst, we could do the presentation without the video. It's not like they know we have it, and no one promised them a great video presentation. We can just wing it without the video. We've got plenty to do this afternoon without tearing apart the department. Of course, I'll help look for it if that's what you all want to do."

As we've seen before, there are positives and negatives to all of the traits that I will talk about. How could there be anything bad about being emotionally stable? If you're like Joe, sometimes you can be a little too stable, a little too laid back. There are times when there is a level of energy that accompanies being nervous and excitable and, yes, even a little neurotic, that can be helpful. Joe doesn't have it.

You handle this situation by saying something like, "Joe, I'm not sure you realize the seriousness of the situation. We may be out of work if we don't come up with a way to prove our value to the new senior staff. We need to spend some time looking for that video, and if we don't find it, we're going to have to brainstorm some creative ways to fill in the information in a different way, and I need your help on that."

EARTHBOUND: CHARACTERISTICS OF HAVING YOUR FEET ON THE GROUND

People who have their feet on the ground tend to be calm, level-headed, and somewhat cautious. They don't act on impulse very often. They tend not to react emotionally in most situations, and they don't seem to get upset very easily. They are very easy to be around, right up until the time they annoy you by being overly placid in the face of what you feel is a crisis they should be paying attention to.

Although they may not be given to fits of anger or depression, they may not show extremes of the more pleasant emotions either. When given a lovely gift or pleasant surprise, they may smile and say, "Thanks." The giver may feel a bit disappointed about not seeing more enthusiasm or excitement.

LOST IN SPACE: CHARACTERISTICS OF BEING CARRIED AWAY

People who get carried away, on the other hand, are very emotionally reactive. To the casual observer, their reactions seem more intense than the average person's, and the minor frustrations of an ordinary day seem very difficult for this individual to handle. They are often characterized as being moody, which means they're often in a bad mood. As a result they suffer a great deal from stress, and unless they've taken steps to learn how to manage it, they cope badly with stress. They tend to be ruled by their emotions and thus are seen as impulsive and uncontrolled.

They may show the other extreme also; that is, they may be very excited at good news and show extreme joy or excitement when given a gift that they appreciate or a pleasant surprise.

EARTHLY COMBINATIONS

Let's look at how these types work together: two-feet-on-the-ground individuals, two carried-away individuals, and one of each.

Two "Feet on the Ground" Individuals

Two "feet on the ground" individuals set to perform a task may actually be a match made in heaven. These two calm, controlled, poised individuals will get to the job at hand, immediately, without distractions. The only problem that may arise is if there is a crisis that requires just a bit of nervous energy that these two people don't possess. See the example of Joe in the case study, who was so calm and collected that he didn't realize how urgent the issue of the missing video really was. A team or duo made up of these individuals might underappreciate an urgent deadline.

Two "Carried Away" Individuals

What will happen with two "carried away" individuals working together? They will actually begin to annoy each other if there is a crisis brewing, because each one feels that he is more pitiful than the other. And they will start to try to outdo each other in the "poor pitiful me" contest. They will lay the work aside and begin the sad life stories or sad work tales. They may begin to try to compete for who is the most overworked, who has the worst life, who has the worst kids, the worst spouse, the most bills, the worst in-laws, etc., and unless they break out of this conversation, they may never get back to the task at hand.

One of Each

When someone who has her "feet on the ground" works with a "carried away" individual, the situation can work out just fine as long as they appreciate each other. And that is a big if. Obviously, the two can also annoy each other a great deal. An individual with her feet on the ground can bring a great deal of calm and poise to the situation and a realistic outlook. The one who gets carried away can bring some nervous energy and a sense of urgency to the situation. Together they can iron out the details and get the job done in a realistic period of time. Once again, the key is to help them understand each other and to appreciate what the other has to bring to the table. How do we do that?

Co-Workers. In the case of two co-workers, it's a matter of coming to appreciate each other's style over time. If you've been working with someone for a period of time, quit being surprised when he reacts in a certain very predictable way, and work with what you know you are going to get from him.

Let's pretend that you know after two years of working with him that your co-worker (let's call him Amal) tends to get carried away. So when he does, be prepared to be empathetic, and then bring him back down to earth. Say something like, "I know, it is frustrating when they keep changing the rules on us like this. Unfortunately, that seems to be the way they like us to do business. Now let's see how we can make this work. I know we can do it because we've done it successfully in the past. And you and I make a great team."

If you are the person frustrated by the "feet on the ground" co-worker, it can be helpful simply to ask that person some questions. Her responses might seem muted to you or you might be tempted to assume that she doesn't care. Ask her! How does she feel about this project? Say something like, "Linda, what are your thoughts on this program? Didn't it make you mad when the boss told us that we had to have this done by Friday instead of next week? What did you think of Sandra's news that she's getting married?" Don't just assume that your "feet on the ground" co-worker doesn't care about any of these things. If you ask some good questions, you may find that the person does indeed have some emotions. She just doesn't express them the way you do.

Boss and Employee. For a boss who has her feet on the ground, it is certainly challenging to work with employees who get carried away. Setting the tone for the organization or the department and clearly communicating every policy and every change is a good start. From the employees' perspective, the boss may seem unimaginative and dull. They might think, "Doesn't she get it? Doesn't she see the problems that surround us? Why isn't she more worried?" For those of you who get carried away, remember that keeping your feet on the ground is not necessarily a bad thing.

Like the co-worker, the boss can remember to be empathetic but has to keep it short and businesslike. Give too much and you are simply playing into their "woe is me" game. A little reverse psychology, carefully applied, can sometimes be helpful. For example, consider the exchange you might have if you were Amal's boss and not his co-worker.

Amal: "Oh no! Not another change in the rules. They are doing it to us again. I can't believe it."

Boss: "I know. It is frustrating when the rules change and we have to learn a new way of doing things. I think we are all going to die now, right?"

Amal: ". . . What?"

Boss: "We're not? Well, what is the worst that is going to happen, then?"

From the employee's perspective, again the questioning technique is the best way to approach the "feet on the ground" boss. For instance, you might ask, "What are the implications of this announcement? How is this going to affect our department? What specifically does this mean for our annual budget numbers?" These are examples of questions to probe what you feel may be a "bad news" announcement that your boss has presented in a kind of a low-key way. If your boss is reacting less than happily to a pleasant situation, feel free to ask questions under those circumstances also: "Are you pleased with the tickets the department got you for your birthday? Would you prefer a different event/a different night/something else altogether?"

Employee and Boss. If the boss is the one who gets carried away on a regular basis, it can be difficult for employees who have their feet on the ground. I worked in an office once where the general atmosphere was one of stress and anxiety. From the boss on down, people bounced off the walls regularly, and I had to work hard to maintain calm and minimize my own stress, only to be misunderstood by this boss. She thought I didn't care and that I lacked a sense of urgency. The fact was, my work was fine. I asked her to judge me by my results and not by my demeanor! I had to negotiate this with her several times before she was able to see through what she saw as a lack of urgency (because it was different from her style) and admit that my work was fine.

The carried-away boss needs to realize that he is not only creating stress in his department (which can lead to a great deal of unintended consequences like sick days and loss of productivity due to high stress levels), but he might keep people from being unable to distinguish a true crisis from an everyday crisis. When everything is a disaster, how can the employees tell when you really mean it this time?

HOW TO BE MORE BALANCED IF YOU'VE GOT YOUR "FEET ON THE GROUND"

As a co-worker, you may not want to be more balanced. You take great pride in being calm, cool, and collected. But keep in mind that if you're surrounded by people who get carried away a lot of the time and you want to be a team player, it wouldn't hurt to show a bit of emotion once in a while if the rest of them are bouncing off the walls quite a bit. Feel free to join them. You don't have to get too carried away, but spend a minute commiserating with them before you bring them back down to earth and say, "Of course, we still have to carry out the new directives, so now let's spend a little bit of time talking about how we're going to do that."

Remember, also, that as a "feet on the ground" individual you tend to underreact to good news in the eyes of some other people. When someone gives you good news, you may want to overdo it a bit in your reaction. Take your cue from how the others around you act, if everyone else seems to be getting a bit "carried away" in your eyes, remember that, in their opinion, that is normal behavior. You don't have to get as carried away as they do, but you may want to exaggerate your own behavior just a little bit and meet them halfway.

As a boss, you have even more latitude in which to bring down those with their heads in the clouds. When people are getting carried away, you certainly want to empathize with them a little bit because you're not going to change their personalities overnight. But you do want to be very clear with them about what their responsibilities and deadlines are.

Also, as a boss, remember that your employees may see your responses as somewhat muted. For example, when you get a birthday gift or holiday gift you may want to exaggerate your reaction just a bit. Chances are, your employees have been disappointed by your reaction in the past. When an employee gives you news of an impending marriage or birth, the same thing applies. If you see other people reacting in a way that seems a bit carried away, keep in mind that those around you may see it as normal behavior. You don't have to match your behavior to theirs exactly, but you may want to exaggerate yours just a bit.

This issue becomes most critical as a boss when you have to deliver very good or very bad news to your employees. Keep in mind that your employees will tend to underestimate the news if you deliver it in your typical "feet on the ground" manner. If you are delivering some very urgent news, you may really need to alter your style of delivery. If you deliver it in your usual "feet on the ground" manner and it is really urgent, your employees may walk away thinking it is no big deal and therefore not tackle the problem with the urgency that it deserves. If this has happened to you, it may very well be that your employees expected you to communicate a little more urgently if there really was a problem. The same applies to very good news. If you have ever made announcements to your employees and been puzzled by their reactions, consider altering the style of your delivery.

As the "feet on the ground" employee, you may have to do what I did when I had a carried-away boss. Remind him once in a while of the work that you do, how you do it, and how well you do it. Remind him that the sense of urgency that he is not seeing really does not affect your work. On the other hand, there are times when you may want to exaggerate your behavior just a bit. You don't want to cause yourself a lot of stress, but you do know the old expression, "When in Rome, do as the Romans do." If you are surrounded by a lot of "carried away" people, it may not hurt to exaggerate your reactions just a bit in the name of fitting in with the department.

HOW TO BE MORE BALANCED IF YOU TEND TO GET CARRIED AWAY

As a co-worker, your tendencies are very ingrained in you and seem quite normal to you. They are going to be very tough to change, and it might be impossible. But think about things just a minute before you respond. Is this really as difficult as it seems? Think a minute before you speak. Listen to how other people are reacting. Think about what you were going to say, and temper it just slightly. For example, if you are going to say, "This is just terrible," try saying, "This might not work," instead. Try looking at your need to be emotional as a possible detractor from your career. If people see you as difficult to work with and your boss sees you as difficult to handle, it can certainly affect your career and your ability to move forward in the organization.

As a boss, again, I know this tendency might be very much a part of you. But think about how this affects the people who work for you. Try to stop and listen once in a while. Think about the things you tend to say and if there is a way to say them a little bit differently. Is there a "feet on the ground" employee whom you find somewhat annoying because of his calm and collected nature? Try to appreciate him instead of finding him annoying. Instead of expressing your opinion on something, ask him his opinion first. This can be a great way to expand your repertoire of responses.

A boss simply does not have the luxury of acting on his emotions all the time. A boss who is moody has a very detrimental impact on his employees. Your employees have their eyes on you all the time. When you come to work in a bad mood, employees wonder why. Instead of going about their productive workday, they may be speaking to one another, gathering around the coffee pot, asking what they did wrong, wondering if something's going wrong with the company, etc. You simply can't afford to be in a bad mood. Think of yourself as a stage actor. You come to work each morning playing the part of the boss. You need to put on that actor's face and put off the bad mood. You can do it. Your mood is your choice. You know how I know? If the big boss or the person you admired most in the world were there that day, or if you were going to a job interview, you would throw off that bad mood very quickly. Don't think of it as just the face you put on for your employees. Think of it as the role you play as a boss and leader, think of how important it is to your employees' productivity, and think of the good of your department and the good of the organization.

Keep in mind that whether she says so or not, you probably can be very annoying to your boss if you are an employee who tends to get carried away. I know, you can't help it. I know it's just the way you are, but think about ways that you can shift some of your thinking. Instead of saying the first thing that comes to mind, bring it down just a notch and say it a little bit differently. When you think about the worst thing that can happen, try to think about what else could happen instead, and state it that way. Ask someone else's opinion about what might happen before you state yours. A reputation as someone who is difficult to handle can have a detrimental effect on your career growth. You are the only one who has immediate control over moods that you are in. Try to think of every day and every meeting as a job interview.

Whether you are a co-worker, boss, or employee, remember what I said about making small changes. I know we're talking about the habits of a lifetime and that changing them is going to be difficult. But think about the old children's story of the boy who cried wolf. He enjoyed terrorizing his village by telling everyone that a wolf was coming to eat them all up. His tale wasn't true, and of course the villagers eventually learned to ignore him. One day the actual wolf showed up, the little boy ran down the street warning everyone, and of course everyone ignored him. And guess what happened? Because children's stories always have a moral to them, you can imagine how it ends: The wolf ate the boy. If everything is a crisis, what happens when there's a real crisis? If everything is a tragedy, how are your co-workers going to react when there is a real tragedy in your life?

 ## WHAT WE'VE LEARNED ON OUR TRIP TO EARTH

Feet on the Ground

Positive Characteristics. A person who has her feet on the ground tends to be emotionally controlled, shows constraint, controls her impulses, is able to reflect on her actions, is level-headed, and is somewhat cautious.

Negative Characteristics. On the other hand, people may see the calm, composed person as not having the sense of urgency that a project or job demands. He may seem unappreciative of good things. He is too mellow; he can come across as not seeming to care too much about the job or task at hand. He may underestimate good news and pleasant surprises, and he may underestimate bad news.

What You Will Get from Them

- Emotional stability

- Calmness

- Poise

What You Need to Give Them

- Credit for caring

- Reality checks

- Questions (what are you feeling?)

Carried Away

Positive Characteristics. The person who tends to get carried away may bring needed energy to a project. When his mood swings to the positive side, he can be fun to have around.

Negative Characteristics. The person whom I have characterized as being carried away will often appear anxious, angry, depressed, or irritable. Other times he might appear inappropriately cheerful, as his emotions tend to be inappropriate to the situation. He will tend to act on impulse.

What You Will Get from Them

* Energy

* Moodiness

* Emotional reactions

What You Need to Give Them

* Reality checks

* Empathy

* Safety

AFTER OUR TRIP TO THE EARTH

This worksheet will help you think about the concepts presented in this chapter.

1. Which end of the spectrum most characterizes me?

Feet on the Ground ← → **Carried Away**

2. How does this trait help me contribute positively to situations?

3. When do I need to "stretch" a bit in the opposite direction?

4. Which end of the spectrum most characterizes those closest to me at work? (If you have chosen to analyze your boss, particular co-workers, and/or employees who are particularly problematic for you at work, continue to analyze that person or persons here.)

MY BOSS

Feet on the Ground ← → **Carried Away**

MY CO-WORKERS

Feet on the Ground ←――――――――――――――――――→ **Carried Away**

MY PEERS

Feet on the Ground ←――――――――――――――――――→ **Carried Away**

MY EMPLOYEES

Feet on the Ground ←――――――――――――――――――→ **Carried Away**

5. How can I best call on these people when I need to use their natural abilities?

6. How can I avoid expecting them to do things that fly in the face of their natural style? How can I stop being disappointed in them or angry at them when they do what just comes naturally to them?

7. How can I change my behavior to get along better with these people?

CHAPTER 5
The Moon Landers

For this chapter, I'm going to change my approach a bit. Rather than discuss people *from* the moon, I'll look at those who traveled *to* the moon. How did they manage to land on the moon—that is, how did they go from the initial vision to the actual landing? It took two kinds of people—two kinds of personality styles. One of the types I will talk about in this chapter are people who are imaginative, intuitive, and like to come up with original ideas. At the other end of the spectrum are people who are concrete thinkers, who focus on the facts at hand, and are very realistic about what can be accomplished.

ISN'T THAT INTERESTING?/THAT'S WRONG

On one end of this spectrum are people who are more *intellectual* (*not* more intelligent). They are *original, curious,* and *imaginative,* although sometimes *unrealistic.* When they hear a new idea or something they do not agree with, they are liable to ask for more information.

The people on the other end of the spectrum tend to be *unre-*

flective and somewhat *narrow-minded*, although they are *stable*, *reliable*, and *consistent*. When presented with a new idea, they are more likely to find problems with it and feel that it is wrong.

BEFORE WE TRAVEL TO THE MOON

What I am talking about here is one of the Big Five personality traits, known as openness to experience. We will relate the people I discuss here to the Jungian typology continuum that includes sensors and intuitors. Sensors like things they can see and touch, and issues they can prove with facts, but intuitors like to rely on their intuition.

People whom I will refer to as the "isn't that interesting?" group love new insights, new possibilities, and working with innovative ideas. They delve into abstract thinking with great enthusiasm. They tend to be future-oriented, and they like ideas for their own sake, not necessarily for their practical value. Sometimes their motto seems to be "This is a great idea; we'll find out what it's good for some other time." They like time for reflection and imagination.

The war starts when the group of co-workers that I am going to talk about next reacts to all of this by saying, "That's wrong." These people are more concrete thinkers who prefer to focus on the facts, who are more realistic, and who think ideas should have some current practical value. Although the designation "that's wrong" may seem a little harsh, these people have plenty of data and facts to back up that conclusion. They don't trust intuition, and they tend to think that the "Isn't that interesting?" crowd is full of impractical dreamers.

Which End of the Spectrum Most Characterizes Me?

Do you tend to be practical and factual in your approach to tasks? Do you take a logical and analytical approach, and is that what you are most comfortable with? Or do you tend to take a more big-picture, questioning approach to tasks and see them in terms of the possibilities they represent?

Which End of the Spectrum Most Characterizes Those Closest to Me at Work: My Boss, My Co-Workers, My Peers, and My Employees?

Have you been reminded of any co-workers yet? Do you have any people around you at work who seem energized by new ideas and whose reactions are, "Yes, and here's another way we could do it . . .", and others who say, "Absolutely not."?

WALKING ON THE MOON: POCKET QUARTERBACK OR SCRAMBLER?

Lorrie was starting to wonder about her decision to job share during her last two years as director of human resources in a large bank. It seemed a great way to ease into retirement. She would be working half-time during her last two years on the job and would be able to retain her benefits. One of her peers in another division was in a similar situation, and he had eagerly agreed to be her job-share partner. They shared an office, and although two desks in an office made for one didn't crowd them a great deal, it was the contrast between the two desks that bothered her. Her desk generally held her computer, a leather-bound notebook, a silver pen, and a calendar desk blotter. George, her job-share partner, had what she had always referred to as a "hurricane desk." He had the same computer that she had, but she could hardly see it due to the yellow sticky notes that almost covered it. His desk was covered with piles of papers, manila folders, interoffice envelopes, and what looked suspiciously like last week's newspaper and a couple of clippings from the latest industry magazines. He had a white board on the wall behind the desk with some scrawls on it that, with some imagination, she made out to be his appointment schedule for the week.

Today was their biweekly half-day overlap meeting. Their job-share arrangement called for them to work alternate weeks, with one half-day overlap every two weeks. Lorrie was determined that this week, only their second meeting, she needed to talk to him about some issues that, left unaddressed, she was sure were going to cause problems.

As George rushed in to the office in his usual animated fashion, he greeted her quite warmly and broke into speech. "You live up north of here too, don't you? Have you tried the new highway bypass? It was just finished a couple of weeks ago. I think I probably saved about 10 minutes in my commute this morning. Of course, that may change once more people discover it. And on my way up from a parking garage, someone was talking about a new coffee cart in the lobby. Great croissants! Here, would you like one?"

"No thanks. I've got quite a few things I want to talk to about this morning, though, George, so why don't we get started. We can certainly do that over coffee, though."

"Sure! Go ahead."

"Well, I've made up this agenda, and if you'd like to add anything to it . . ."

"Oh, I'm not much for agendas. I'll just interject as we go along."

So Lorrie took a deep breath and began. "Well, if you look around the office, you can see that you and I have two very different styles of working. I'm just concerned that it might be a bit confusing to the office staff. I like to know exactly what's going on every day, and I've got everything in my calendar in the computer. In fact, our assistant has access to my calendar, and she knows where I am and what I've got going on every day. She makes a copy of my calendar in the morning, gives me one, and she keeps a copy. So anyone who wants to get in touch with me knows exactly where I am or can get in touch with me through her. If something unexpected comes up, I know when I have room in my day to handle it and exactly when I'll be able to return the critical phone calls. I guess you don't even use the computer calendar, right? And like I said, that can be confusing to the employees, and certainly to our assistant, if we do things that differently."

George finished his croissant in one last big bite and swallowed the last of his coffee. He crumpled the cup and shot it toward the trash can. "Lorrie, do you follow football? I know you and your husband have been to some games, right? What you are is a pocket quarterback. You're leading the team by the book. When you're given the ball, you fall back into the pocket and think about which play in the playbook you are using. You throw the ball to a place downfield, where no one might be at the moment, but you know they're going to be there by the time the ball gets there because you've planned it that way in advance. It's in the book, or in your case the computer, and you know that they're going to be there to pick it up for you. It's safe. It's planned, and you're comfortable with that.

"I'm what's known as the scrambler quarterback. I don't stay in the protection of the pocket. The planned plays are fine, but they don't always work. I play with intuition, and if I see some better way to do it, I go for it. In fact I run with the ball myself if I need to. No, I don't want someone going into my calendar and making appointments for me. How do I know what might come up the rest of the day? How do I know what crisis might arise that needs my attention immediately? It makes me very nervous to think of someone else having the ability to come in and commit parts of my day for me when I have responsibilities to people all over this region."

"How are we going to make this work, then?" asked Lorrie. "People are going to go crazy if they are handled with one style one week and a very different style the next week."

"Trust me," said George. "It happens every weekend in football games. The teams get to know their quarterbacks. If the starting quarterback is a good pocket man, the team knows that and it plays accordingly. If the starting quarterback is out for a while and they put in the backup man who's a scrambler, the team adjusts and it works just as well for that person. We'll make this work, partner. Now I need another croissant. Want one?"

With those words George was out the door. Lorrie was not convinced, and her agenda was not finished! Can this partnership be saved?

FLY ME TO THE MOON: CHARACTERISTICS OF THE "ISN'T THAT INTERESTING?" PERSON

As I said at the outset of the chapter, those people whose motto is "Isn't that interesting?" tend to be more intellectual (not more intelligent) than others. That means that they have an appreciation for new ideas, and unusual ideas, and they tend to show a lot of imagination and curiosity. They are sometimes seen as holding unconventional or individualistic beliefs. They are often proud of marching to the beat of a different drummer. They see themselves as flexible and can take that to an extreme, often introducing change just for the sake of change or stirring things up just to see if something new might be better.

They trust their hunches. We can only speculate as to why this is so, but it probably has a lot to do with the fact that this personality trait, like all the ones I've been talking about, tends to have been with us from birth. When people are intuitive and like it, they learn to trust their intuition. So if I have an intuitive nature, then I learn to trust my feelings. I learn to say, "That's interesting," in response to a new and unusual idea because in the past that has paid off for me.

At work, you can imagine that these people can quickly become bored with the same old routine and doing the same job over and over again. They like to learn new things and like to become involved in creative work, brainstorming, and coming up with new ideas. They become so challenged by a new and complicated problem, and so excited by having new insights, that they bring a lot of excitement and energy to a team. They can overlook some of the facts and constraints along the way. They are bored by standard operating procedures. They prefer change, sometimes drastic change, to the simple continuation of day-to-day routine. Obviously, in some jobs, there can be a downside to this. They can become the organizational maverick, and in some organizations and in some jobs, a loose cannon is not the best thing to have around. People sometimes see them as impractical or too theoretical.

BLUE MOON: CHARACTERISTICS OF THE "THAT'S WRONG" PERSON

The people who have "That's wrong" as their motto tend to be fairly conventional and tend to have narrow interests. They prefer facts and solid data. They do not get excited over complicated and ambiguous problems. They prefer to deal with plain and straightforward issues. They tend not to gravitate toward the arts and pure sciences, seeing these things as having no real practical value. They prefer the familiar to the novel and may resist change.

These people do not necessarily trust their hunches. They trust their conscious thought and like to dig into the detail of the situation rather than sit back and wonder about the possibilities. To them, that is the only real way to get to the truth and the real solution to a problem. They have no desire to change the world or to innovate, they want to focus on what is real and practical, and they want to solve the immediate problem at hand when they are faced with a task.

They like using their experience and what has happened in the past to solve problems. They like standard operating procedures. They enjoy applying skills that they already have and at which they are already competent. They like the facts, and they seldom make errors in their dealings with facts. But they rarely have creative inspirations and wouldn't trust them if they did. They like to do things that have practical application. They like to continue doing what works, maybe with some fine tuning, but not with leaps of logic or with making any drastic changes.

Of course, the "isn't that interesting?" group may see them as shortsighted. Instead of looking at the big picture or the possibilities, they are busy looking at the logic and pursuing things in a clear sequence from start to finish. Nothing could be more boring and less interesting to the other group.

LUNAR COMBINATIONS

And that brings us to how the combinations work together. As always, there are challenges whether you have two of the same type or one of each in groups.

Two "Isn't That Interesting?" People

These two will take a great deal of pleasure in working together. Whether they are productive or not depends on the task. They will be creative, will brainstorm a great deal, will be innovative, and will come up with a great many new and exciting ideas. Is that a good thing or not? If they are working on a very detailed, repetitive task that must be done in a certain way, due perhaps to regulatory compliance issues, then no, this is decidedly not a very good thing. But working in a marketing department and coming up with a new and innovative ad campaign is an excellent task for them to be working on together.

Two "That's Wrong" People

On the other hand, two people who agree to take practical, fact-based approaches to all tasks would do extremely well on the detailed, repetitive tasks based on regulatory compliance. They would dig into a task, get it done, and enjoy the fact that it has parameters, details, and deadlines. They would, in fact, do poorly at creating an advertising campaign because it would ask them to brainstorm and be innovative—so much so that it would be unusual to find them in such a situation and unlikely that anyone would charge them with such a task a second time.

One of Each

When we find one of each, we are both blessed and cursed. In all of the combinations that we have looked at so far, I have pointed out that the combinations can work well or they can be grounds for all-out conflict. This certainly is true in this case, and this is where the moon landing can go terribly wrong and miss its mark by millions of miles. If ever there were a case where two types of personalities were almost speaking different languages—truly aliens in the workplace—this would be the case. They simply can't understand each other without some real work put in to understanding. Let's take a look at how this might play out.

Co-Workers. Boss: "Why didn't this order get processed yesterday? It was supposed to be on my desk this morning."

Martha: "The copier broke down again. You know, I was reading about this new generation of copiers. Instead of jamming all the time, they have a new kind of feed mechanism and supposedly they never break down, at least the way ours do. There is no jamming, anyway. And you know . . ."

Now here's how a different employee might react in the same situation.

Boss: "Sam, why didn't the order get processed yesterday?"

Sam: "The copier broke down at four o'clock. We called the repair company, but they had already closed for the day. I took the lid off the machine and tried to break the jam, but it looks as if the jam was in too deep; beyond what I could reach by taking the screws off. So I put it back together. The repair call is for 10 o'clock this morning, and I asked for Ravi, who was here last time and was able to get it fixed in about 15 minutes. So I'm thinking the order will be on your desk by 11 at the latest."

And off go Martha and Sam to another day of working together. How do you think it might go? Actually, once again, it depends on the task. Certainly they have the ability to annoy each other. But if they could learn to appreciate each other, they might work together fairly effectively. Give them the innovative advertising campaign task and Sam would certainly need Martha on his team in order to be effective. He could take care of the details, the agenda, and keeping them on schedule. And she could do the creative work. If they had learned to appreciate and use each other's talents, they could make a great team. What about the detailed, repetitive tasks based on regulatory compliance? Martha would need Sam on her team to keep her in line, but is there even a place for Martha on those tasks? If they were indeed part of the job, Martha may simply have to be reined in and kept in line; if they were the sole responsibility of the job, Martha may find she is a bad fit for the job and will probably (voluntarily or involuntarily) be looking for other work.

Boss and Employee. If you are a boss who tends to be an innovative "isn't that interesting?" kind of a person, keep in mind that it's a fine way to be, right up until the time it quits working for you. If you have a lot of employees who are detailed, practical, and fact-focused, they may frustrate you. Instead, you may want to remind yourself to be grateful for them. They bring a much-needed extra set of competencies to your team. There are times when it pays to be detailed, practical, and fact-focused. Learn to recognize those times and call on those employees to do the detail work that you are simply not all that interested in and, frankly, not even that good at.

What if you have a boss who is always being innovative and creative and you are frustrated because you like to stick to the facts? Quit doing what hasn't worked in the past. In other words, quit bringing her reams of facts. Quit hoping that she will change and one day wake up and say, "Oh, I see, you're right!" That isn't the way she thinks. Do what you do best, and find a way to remind your boss of that. See if you can find a way to relieve her of tasks like scheduling, paperwork, and things that have frustrated you in the past because they have fallen through the cracks. Present it as a way for you to grow your skills and as a way for her to free up some of her own time. She will appreciate it because it is drudgery to her, and you will get to do work that you are very good at and will be appreciated for come performance-review time.

Employee and Boss. If you are the practical, detailed, fact-focused boss, yes, you also will be frustrated if you find yourself surrounded by innovative, creative people. And once again, it will behoove you to find a way to foster an appreciation of them. As I said in the "Boss and Employee" section, they bring a much-needed competency to your team. You will need to develop the ability to recognize when innovation and creativity are needed and tap into your employees for their help in those kinds of tasks. Then be open to their ideas.

If you are the innovative, creative employee working for the practical, fact-based boss, it is a bit harder to identify ways to be of service to him. Be alert for times when he may be frustrated or stuck; for instance, perhaps he has been asked to come up with new ideas for a fund-raiser or asked to serve on a task force for a new customer service campaign. Those are times to offer to meet and brainstorm with him; you can show your stuff and give him lots of material for his meeting! Depending on your position, you may even offer to take his place in the task force.

HOW TO BE MORE BALANCED IF YOU'RE AN "ISN'T THAT INTERESTING?" PERSON

I said earlier that sensors and intuitors, perhaps more than any of the other types, tend to speak almost different languages.

Because of that, it is important that when you are trying to be more balanced, whether as a co-worker, a boss, or an employee, that you take the time to learn the other person's language by asking questions. As an innovative, creative person, ask practical fact-based questions like: "What are the facts of the matter as you see them? What exactly is the situation right now; can you lay it out for me? What already exists, what works?" This is sensing language, and sensors will respect you for asking. Once a sensor has had a chance to tell you all these things, and you respect her in return by taking careful notes, then perhaps you can gently lead her in the direction you want to go. You have laid the groundwork by listening to her and can now ask her permission to go in your direction.

How exactly is this making you more balanced? Remember you are not just asking the questions in order to kill time to have your turn to talk. You are listening, and hopefully you are learning. If you are an extreme case of "isn't that interesting?", you are learning a few things about the positive aspects of the "that's wrong" people. And I hope you are learning a new respect for what those other people are like.

As always, as a co-worker you have less power than when you are a boss. You have to tread a bit lightly when you are trying to change your peers' behavior because you are in an equal position with those people. Share with them what you have learned from this chapter. Don't just sneak up on them with the questions I suggested. Ask them if they'd be willing to cooperate with you and negotiate a better working relationship.

As a boss, you need to do two things. You need to recognize that you are an "isn't that interesting?" kind of person, and you need to find people around you, among your peers, or on your team who do have the "that's wrong" trait. Draw on them as needed. Also remember to learn from them as you are drawing on their strengths. There may be times when you don't have them around you, and you may have to act a little bit more like them in order to get what you need from a certain situation.

As an employee, you also need to tread a bit lightly. Be very alert for opportunities to show your boss that your different style can actually be an asset to her. Once you have done that a time or two, she will begin to pick up on such opportunities herself. Learn that at times you may need to act more like her in order to get along in certain circumstances. You can be just as practical as she is.

HOW TO BE MORE BALANCED IF YOU'RE A "THAT'S WRONG" PERSON

As I said, it is important to try to learn the other person's language. When you are the practical, fact-based person who is working with the creative and innovative person, begin by asking him the following types of questions: "What insights do you have about the situation? What are your hunches here? What other possibilities might there be? What interpretations do you make from these facts?" These are the kinds of questions this person loves, and he should respond very eagerly. Pay close attention, take notes, and let him speak freely until he is done. Then you can lead him gently in the direction of what you want to talk about. And he ought to return the favor. In fact, don't be afraid to ask him directly to return the favor by letting you now talk freely about the things that are of interest to you.

Remember also that you can learn a few things about the positive aspects of the intuitive trait as you do this. There are times when it pays to be more like this person, and you can use these conversations as a learning tool for yourself.

As a co-worker, negotiate the situation and share with him what you know now about the best ways you two can work together. Ask him the questions and request that he then ask you questions from the "How to Be More Balanced If You're an 'Isn't That Interesting?' Person" section. Remember to learn from him as you go. If you are an extreme "that's wrong" person, this will be hard, but try to understand that there will be situations when you may be called upon to give an opinion in a meeting on a creative topic, and a bit of practice at it now will make you look better and more well-rounded in the long run.

As a boss, you probably already know very well whether you're a "that's wrong" kind of person, and you also need to find people around you, among your peers or on your team, who are different and whom you can draw on as needed. Also remember to learn from them as you are drawing on their strengths. I know it will feel funny and will go against the grain with you, but it will put new tools in your toolbox if you can at least learn to speak the language of creativity and innovation.

As an employee, be very alert for opportunities to show your boss that your different style can actually be an asset to her. Take those mundane tasks that she doesn't want to do anyway. She'll be happy to turn them over to you and will be quick to pick up on more opportunities to do so, once you get the ball rolling. As I said in the other examples though, at times you may need to act more like her. Some day when you're in a meeting and someone asks that terrible question, "Who wants to brainstorm about this?" you won't panic!

 ## WHAT WE'VE LEARNED ON OUR TRIP TO THE MOON

"Isn't That Interesting?"

Positive Characteristics. The people who have the motto "Isn't that interesting?" are full of ideas. They are intellectually curious and imaginative. They use and trust their intuition and like to follow their hunches.

Negative Characteristics. Their tendency to be speculative can come across as dreamy and impractical. They can be flexible to the point of being organizational mavericks or "loose cannons." Their ideas can be unrealistic.

What You Will Get from Them

- New ideas
- A desire to learn new skills
- New insights
- Foresight

What You Need to Give Them

- The big-picture, the overview
- Patience

- Encouragement of imagination
- Time for reflection

"That's Wrong"

Positive Characteristics. The people who have the motto "That's wrong" are stable and practical. They are reliable, consistent, and realistic and like to focus on the facts at hand.

Negative Characteristics. They can be also be unreflective and somewhat narrow-minded, and they sometimes tend to resist needed change.

What You Will Get from Them

- Facts
- Reliability
- Excellence at their established skills
- Orientation toward the present

What You Need to Give Them

- Facts, details, and examples
- A well-thought-out plan
- A logical sequence of steps to a task

AFTER OUR TRIP TO THE MOON

This worksheet will help you think about the concepts presented in this chapter.

1. Which end of the spectrum most characterizes me?

Isn't That Interesting? ⟵——————⟶ That's Wrong

2. How does this trait help me contribute positively to situations?

3. When do I need to "stretch" a bit in the opposite direction?

4. Which end of the spectrum most characterizes those closest to me at work? (If you have chosen to analyze your boss, particular co-workers, and/or employees who are particularly problematic for you at work, continue to analyze that person or persons here.)

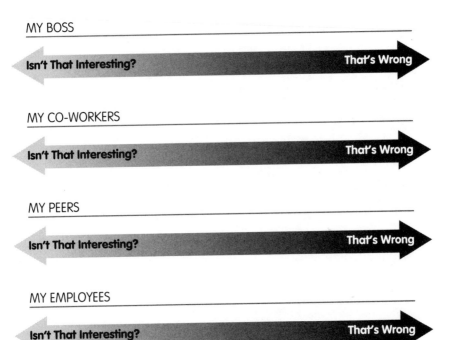

MY BOSS

Isn't That Interesting?   That's Wrong

MY CO-WORKERS

Isn't That Interesting?   That's Wrong

MY PEERS

Isn't That Interesting?   That's Wrong

MY EMPLOYEES

Isn't That Interesting?   That's Wrong

5. How can I best call on these people when I need to use their natural abilities?

6. How can I avoid expecting them to do things that fly in the face of their natural style? How can I stop being disappointed in them or angry at them when they do what just comes naturally to them?

7. How can I change my behavior to get along better with these people?

CHAPTER 6
Martian Colleagues

The planet Mars is named after the god of war. In our language, we have often used the word *Martian* to stand for someone who is antagonistic to the standard homelike values of earth. People sometimes attribute anything foreign, hard to understand, or bizarre to the "Martians." And because I am talking about conflict in this book (personality conflict in particular), I will take the severe warlike form of conflict, and the planet god who represents it, to discuss a trait that is as difficult to deal with as any we have seen so far.

THE DOMINANT ONES/THE COMPLIANT ONES

Have you ever dealt with someone who clearly wanted to win at all costs? Seemingly impervious to any logical arguments, she will often take the contrary view in what seems to be an automatic fashion. Others are more likely to give in gracefully and seem honestly to not care much whether they win a game or an argument.

Those people who *give in gracefully* have a *low need for power,* show what is called *social humility,* and are *cooperative* and *com-*

pliant in conflict. The other type, with a *high need for power*, are much more *dominant* and *argumentative in conflict* and possibly comes across as *arrogant*.

BEFORE WE TRAVEL TO MARS

For research on this trait, we look to McClelland's theory of motivation, the one that divides our needs into affiliation, achievement, and power. The person whose need for power is high is clearly motivated by different things and acts differently than someone whose need for power is low.

Someone with a high need for power will sometimes seem to argue just for the sake of argument. He seems to not only want, but really needs, to get his own way. And he doesn't seem to distinguish between minor and major issues. Issues like what day the strategy meeting is held on and what chair he gets to sit in seem to be as important to him as the decisions made at the meeting about the company's newest five-year strategy.

People with a lower need for power will give in gracefully; but if they are too low on this trait, they sometimes give in too gracefully. Because someone who is too low on this trait may not care at all if he gets his way, he sometimes doesn't fight hard enough for his opinion.

Which End of the Spectrum Most Characterizes Me?

Does it seem that most days at work are full of battles—The Cubicle Wars—to be fought and won? Are you always burning with what seems like a righteous indignation to get things settled in a fair and equitable manner? Or are you reasonably calm and don't really feel a need to control how things get solved?

Which End of the Spectrum Most Characterizes Those Closest to Me at Work: My Boss, My Co-Workers, My Peers, and My Employees?

What about the people around you at work? Are there people who seem to want to argue over every trivial detail? Is there a person, or more than one, who seems to want to win at all costs, whether it is over minor or major details? On the other hand, are there people who annoy you by giving in quickly on every detail rather than being willing to engage in a debate that could be constructive?

Let's talk about how to deal with people at both ends of the spectrum.

THE ENERGY-SUCKING CO-WORKERS FROM MARS

Judith Whalen, the director of technology for a small software company, looked around the table at her managers. Present were Jack, the accounting manager; Faraah, the customer service manager; Carlos, the warehouse manager; Takuro, the new development manager; and Denisha, the human resources manager.

Judith said, "Because the end of the year is approaching, we need to get together to talk about goals and objectives for next year. We need to set a date within the next week or so for a half-day meeting. I've received the latest company strategy from corporate, and we'll need to go over that and talk about how our objectives can support theirs. How does next Wednesday afternoon look for everyone?"

"Can we make it Thursday instead?" asked Jack. There were a few sighs and a bit of discreet eye rolling from the others, but everyone flipped their electronic calendars to Thursday.

When Thursday arrived, Judith, Faraah, and Carlos had already arrived in the conference room for the one o'clock meeting when Jack walked in. Jack said to Carlos, "Would you mind if I took that chair? I can hear better, and the sun gets in my eyes if I sit anywhere else. Thanks." Carlos moved to another chair.

When everyone arrived, Judith began the meeting by saying, "I sent you all the strategy statement from corporate regarding the direction they're pursuing for next year. Obviously, our goals and objectives need to align with . . ."

Jack interrupted with, "Yeah, about that. Some of the things they're doing really don't make any sense. Can we let them know that with the direction the industry's going, they really need to . . ."

"Jack, they are not asking for our input," said Judith. "This is a one-way communication from corporate. Next year's strategy is a done deal. Our job today is to figure out what we're going to do to support this from our end. We need to move forward from here. Now let's go around the table and get everyone's input. I'd like to hear everyone's ideas on our goals and objectives for next year. Let's start with Denisha."

"One of the things corporate said is that they want 10 percent of our growth to come from unique products next year," said Denisha. "We need to think about whether that means hiring some people with very different skills than what our current employees have or arranging for some extensive training for our current employees. With our heavy workload, I think it makes more sense to hire some people with very different skills, very soon."

"Oh no," said Jack. "That isn't right at all. We always seem to have a slow time right after the first of the year. And we have a lot of very bright people. We could send them to training, no problem. I don't agree with hiring new people."

"Well, that makes sense too," said Denisha. "I could go along with that."

"Denisha," said Judith, "We need your ideas. Please tell me more about why you think we should hire new employees. That's what we're here for."

MARS ATTACKS: CHARACTERISTICS OF THE DOMINANT ONES

Dominant people come across as having a great deal of confidence. They are handy to have in the room during a tough negotiation, as they do not like to back down. They often assume positions of authority, whether they are the legitimate authority in the room (the manager) or not. They tend to be the first to speak up in a meeting, the first to voice their opinions, and they actively try to influence other people's opinions.

Dominant people risk looking overly aggressive in conflict. They often come across as stubborn, arrogant, annoying, or difficult to be around. They also come across as competitive and as striving to win at all costs. They want to run things, including the most casual conversations. They make statements instead of expressing opinions or asking questions and thus can seem pompous or rude. They will sometimes even not admit to making a mistake or having a lack of knowledge on a given topic.

Although dominant people will sometimes collaborate with colleagues, it is not for any altruistic reason but usually to serve some reason of their own.

Dominant people like outward signs of power, and they like organizations where they are rewarded with promotions, plaques, big offices, company cars, etc. They are likely to display these signs prominently as well. They will often not stay in an organization where they are not recognized, promoted, or given these signs of status. If they do stay, they will fall into the habit of being a chronic complainer.

MY FAVORITE MARTIAN: CHARACTERISTICS OF THE COMPLIANT ONES

Compliant people tend to be easy to get along with. They are cooperative in conflict situations and defer to the needs or requests of other people fairly readily. When they disagree, they will either keep silent or raise their points as questions to consider rather than state their disagreements clearly.

Compliant people tend to be loyal and dependable employees. They readily accept orders and do not have a problem with authority, so managers tend to have no problems with the compliant person until it gets too far down the continuum, such as in the example with Denisha.

That is because, as with all of the traits in this book, being compliant is not all positive. These people may come across as overly submissive, as people who will not stand up for what they believe, and they may annoy others with their social humility. They may be seen as someone from whom it is impossible to get a straight answer. When they have good ideas, they quickly give them up in the face of even the merest hint of opposition, so something that could be of help to the organization or department is lost.

MARTIAN COMBINATIONS

And what happens with the combinations? Let's take a look at two compliant people at work, two dominant ones, and one of each.

Two Compliant People

Two compliant people can work together very effectively as long as they are not too low in their need for power. They are good at collaborating and will hear each other out when discussing a problem or decision. Two reasonably compliant people, in fact, will make a great team. There will be an even amount of give-and-take in the decision-making process, and they will have about an equal amount of input into the decision or the task.

If the two are overly compliant, however, problems will arise because each will be too eager to defer to the other. They will need to be careful to put some kind of an agenda in place that allows both of them to define their ideas and agree upon a structured way to resolve differences of opinion.

Two Dominant People

Two dominant people, on the other hand, will generally have a great deal of difficulty working together right from the start. Each will state an opinion, neither will listen to the other, the exchange will get a bit heated, and things may go downhill from there. This is a difficult situation because a manager may need to step in and give them very specific directions as to how to complete their task or make their decision, and neither of these people like to take direction or receive specific instructions from managers. A manager may simply need to put one of the two "in charge" of the project if there is not a lot of need for collaboration. If there is, any type of structured meeting agenda that allows the two to put their ideas on the table and allows for an even amount of give-and-take can be helpful.

A simple example of such an agenda for two compliant people or two dominant people working together may look like this.

8:00   Presentation of the problem: define all parameters
8:15   Person A: describe all ideas, theories, etc. with respect to solving this issue while Person B takes notes.
8:30   Person B: describe all ideas, theories, etc. with respect to solving this issue while Person A takes notes.
8:45   Person B has an opportunity to respond to Person A's ideas and theories on a point-by-point basis: Agree? Disagree? Why or why not?

9:00   Person A has an opportunity to respond to Person B's ideas and theories on a point-by-point basis: Agree? Disagree? Why or why not?

This can also work well with a compliant person working with a dominant person, but that situation brings with it some unique challenges as well. Let's explore that a bit more next.

One of Each

We need to pay special attention to the dynamic between dominant and compliant people. When the compliant types have good ideas, they often need special handling to get them out on the table or else the dominant types will steamroll those ideas right out of existence. Let's look at the combinations below to see how we can handle these dynamics.

Co-Workers. Imagine Jack and Denisha, from our opening case study, working on a task together. Jack will take the lead, Denisha will follow his every suggestion, and the job will get done. It may even get done very well. But it will get done Jack's way, and Jack's suggestions and opinions will be the only ones that matter. This may or may not be a problem, but on many teams it could very well be an issue. The reason teams exist is often because two heads are better than one; that is, the synergy of creativity and the double-checking that members can do with each other is very helpful.

If you find yourself working with a Jack, what can you do to work around his personality? Remember, what is important to him is winning. If you are careful, you can let him think that he has won and he will be happy. It may bother you a bit at first, but unless you have a high need for power also (and the higher your need, the more it will bother you) you can learn this technique easily. And if it does bother you, try thinking of it as another way of winning.

The way you are going to do this is to plant ideas in Jack's mind. Be subtle about it, but say things like, "Jack, I think you're right about that." (You are actually talking about something you mentioned the other day and he was only vaguely supportive of.) Keep stressing the fact, over time, that it was his idea and what a good idea it was. Jack's ego will take over and he will take credit for it. Praise Jack; remember, that is what he lives for. Don't overdo it, but over the course of several days, keep dropping subtle remarks like:

"Jack's idea about XYZ seems like the best way to go . . ."

"I really like what Jack said the other day about . . ."

"Jack, tell us more about . . ." (Ask him about something you know is in his area of expertise.)

I know, it feels wrong! But you will win in the long run, the team wins, the idea gets adopted, or the task gets done.

Now, what if the opposite is the case? What if you are working with Denisha on a project and want to draw her out? Remember, she is overly compliant and simply agrees immediately with whatever is suggested. The best tactic with an overly compliant person is never to state your own opinion first. Note that in our opening case study, when Judith said she was going to go around the table and get everyone's opinion, she began with Denisha. She undoubtedly knew from past experience that Denisha was highly compliant and unless asked first would simply agree with whatever was said. Structure discussions with these people carefully; get them to tell you everything they think before you give them even a hint of your own opinion on the subject.

Boss and Employee. What if the boss is the dominant person and he has compliant employees? This almost seems like the stereotypical boss-employee relationship. And it may or may not be a problem. The boss has the power, the boss gives the orders, and the compliant employees follow them. The problem may be found within the broader organization, and a serious problem or crisis may surface that costs the organization an important customer or a great deal of money. For example, it might turn out that an employee, or more than one employee, knew there was a problem but never said anything to solve it. Why? He was never asked. A compliant employee is not going to speak up on his own. And a dominant boss is not in the habit of asking his employees' opinions. A dominant boss with compliant employees may experience one or two crises like this before he realizes that he needs to take a more collaborative approach with his employees.

The compliant employees may need to be a bit subtle in their approach to getting their voices heard with a dominant boss, just as the co-workers were with Jack. It helps if the boss has a bit of a big ego that can be stroked (as many tend to have) or is busy (as so many managers tend to be). The compliant employee can carefully say things like, "I was thinking about that idea you had the other day, boss, and I think it was just great!" The boss may vaguely remember discussing the idea in the meeting, and being praised for having the idea may work for a dominant, ego-driven, busy boss. This is risky and should not be used too often, but a compliant employee doesn't have a lot to lose by trying this one from time to time. The lesson here is that when it best serves you, *let the boss think he has won*, and you will win in the long run.

Actually, a dominant manager can be a very good boss and an effective leader. There isn't anything wrong with having this need for power. Having power allows one to attain management positions and accomplish management tasks. The best managers, though, once they have gotten to their positions of power, realize that they must share this power a little with their employees.

There is another issue here to address, and that is when the dominant boss takes credit for his employees' work. It is one thing to get your way by letting the boss think he has won, and it is quite another to have your hard work and accomplishments virtually stolen from you. When that happens continually, it can hurt not only your self-esteem but your career. And you certainly don't feel like contributing to that by letting your boss think he's won on a day-to-day basis. If this is what's going on, you may need to fight back a bit by playing the politics of that yourself. You may need to become a little more dominant, get your name in lights, and take credit for your accomplishments, even if that means going over your boss's head to ensure you get credit for what you've accomplished.

Employee and Boss. Compliant managers are going to find dominant employees difficult to deal with. A dominant employee does not automatically defer to a manager simply based on title. Dominant employees are liable to be argumentative and will still speak up and give their opinions, whether it is to the president of the company or a fellow employee. Like Jack in our opening case study, they will not hesitate to give their opinions of the corporate strategy any more than they would hesitate to give their opinions of a fellow employee's choice of lunch. To a manager, this can obviously appear as condescending or even insubordinate. The dominant employee has no intention of appearing condescending or rude, because in his mind he's just trying to help. In fact, he probably expects the manager to show him special treatment in recognition of his helpfulness.

A manager's response in this case probably depends on the actual helpfulness of this person. Does your "Jack" actually have expertise that is a help to you? Setting aside his annoying qualities for the moment, if you can, do thank him when he is helpful to you. Do let him know that he is of value to you. Do give him special recognition, as all of these things are the things that he values and craves. If, however, this person is simply a dominant individual who is not of any special value to you, you need to let him know that he is not the manager and that his actions are actually hindering the work group. You can use your managerial power to stop him from derailing the group, much as Judith did in our opening case study, when she cut Jack off when he wanted to derail the group into a discussion of the corporate strategy. Notice that she didn't waste her energy fighting every battle with Jack; did it really matter what chair he sat in? Even the day the meeting was held on, unless it really does matter to Judith, may not be worth fighting about. It seems that Judith has learned to choose her battles carefully with him, but when it is time to step up, shut him down, and keep him from derailing the meeting, she doesn't hesitate to do so.

HOW TO BE MORE BALANCED IF YOU'RE COMPLIANT

If you've read this far and you've recognized yourself as someone who tends to give in a little too easily, you may wonder, "What's wrong with that? So I'm an easy-going person. So I'm flexible. Isn't that better than being arrogant and rude?" Sure it is. Just remember, like everything else I've talked about, every strength can become a weakness. Even if you're just a little bit too compliant, and even if it's only once in a while, you may want to think about times when you can be a little bit more balanced and just a bit more effective at work.

As a co-worker, be aware of your tendency to give in. When it's a matter of where you're going for lunch that day, it may not be a big deal. You need to realize, however, that after a while it can be annoying to your co-workers when, day after day, you are refusing to make decisions. When your co-workers ask you where you'd like to have lunch and your reply is, "I don't care," next time be prepared with a response. Try saying, "Let's go to Julio's for Mexican food," or whatever one of the usual places may be. Then you can move up to stating some bolder opinions in meetings.

You also need to be aware of your tendency to comply too readily. When you do state an opinion in meetings and someone disagrees with you, what is your reaction? Many compliant people think they have only two choices: Give in immediately or fight. Because they don't like to fight, they give in immediately. You do have other choices! Try saying things like, "I understand what you're saying, but I think my idea has merits as well. Let's see if we can come up with a happy medium."

As a compliant boss, it is important that you become more balanced. You have a duty to the organization and to your own bosses to do what you are hired to do; that is, manage your area with your own skills and abilities at the forefront. You cannot allow dominant employees to overpower you. It is going to take some practice, but you can use some of the techniques that I've talked about already to attain a more balanced state. When people ask for your opinion, give it. State your opinion in more forthright terms, even if you're not asked. Compliant people often ask a question instead of making a statement, and that comes across as less dominant. When dealing with dominant people, especially when they are your employees, choose your battles but do not allow them to undermine your authority. Let them know, as Judith did with Jack in our opening case study, when their input is not required.

As a compliant employee, it is going to be difficult to change your style, but you need to recognize when your input is required. If you have a dominant boss, it is very easy to just walk away when a boss gives you orders that you question. You may have fallen into the trap of thinking you had two choices: following the orders without question or challenging him. Again, as I said earlier, there are other choices. Remember, the dominant person likes to be in charge and likes to feel powerful. So begin by letting him feel that way. Say, "That sounds great, boss. I have a question, if you don't mind. I know you know a lot about this. Didn't you tell me once that if we did it this way, we were going to be out of out of compliance with general order number 382? I'd hate to see us get into trouble with corporate." Can you see how you are very subtly giving him credit for coming up with this idea ("didn't you tell me once")? He may or may not have ever told you; the point is you know that what he just told you to do is in direct opposition to one of the corporate directives.

HOW TO BE MORE BALANCED IF YOU'RE DOMINANT

All right, now we come to the hard part! If you are a dominant person, especially if you are pretty high up there on the continuum of the need for power, you are reading this thinking, "But I am right! They should listen to me more! I should not change, they should change!" There are a lot of things in life that should happen but don't. Sometimes the more you fight for something, the more people become defensive and fight back. It can be frustrating and annoying, but the more you feel you're right, the less you get your way. If you can learn to be a little more subtle and a little less obvious, you may be able to get your way more often. By that I mean you can be more effective in the long run, collaborate with people, and meet your own objectives and those of the organization.

If you are a dominant co-worker, I would suggest that you learn to buy yourself some time before you quickly jump in and say things like, "That's a bad idea," or, "That's the wrong thing to do." I know these reactions are more or less second nature to you because so many of the people around you have bad ideas and are wrong. But I promise you, telling them so simply angers them and makes them stop listening to you. So when you use phrases like that and then follow them up with your ideas, people are no longer listening; that's why your good ideas so often don't get heard. So how are you going to change that? How are you going to become more balanced in your communication style so that your ideas can be heard more and you can be more effective at work?

You can buy yourself some time by saying things like, "Interesting," or "I've never thought of it that way before," or "Tell me more about . . ." I know this is going to be very difficult. Write these phrases down on a piece of paper or a sticky note and take them to your next meeting if you have to. They should be the first things out of your mouth when you disagree with what someone says. Let the person talk, ask him more about his ideas, and use a technique called paraphrasing to make sure that you truly understand what it is he is saying. For example, in our opening case study, Jack could have said to Denisha, "So you think that our current employees don't have the ability to come up with unique new products for the market, even if they receive some specialized training? What kind of employees do you think we would need to hire, and where would we need to recruit and hire?" With this kind of question, Denisha feels that Jack is at least taking her opinion seriously before he tells her it is a bad idea. And you know, Jack might even learn something from her response.

As a dominant boss with compliant employees, the biggest lesson to learn from this chapter is a simple one: Don't state your opinion first and then ask your employees what they think. They will simply agree with you. Do what Judith did in the opening case study: Go around the table and ask for opinions from the employees or use other brainstorming techniques. It is up to you to create an environment where employees feel free to state their opinions. You can also put these phrases into your vocabulary when employees approach you with ideas or suggestions: "Interesting," or "I've never thought of it that way before," or "Tell me more about . . ."

As a dominant employee, try to recognize those times when your boss really needs your input and those times when she really doesn't. I know this is going to be difficult to do. If you are really unhappy about the amount of recognition you are receiving for your expertise, go after that next promotion. If the next promotion is eluding you for some reason, do a little soul-searching about why. It is possible, you know, that your expertise is not quite as extensive as you think it is. Depending upon your relationship with your boss, it may be possible to have a heart-to-heart conversation where you can compare notes on how you see your contributions to the department with how she sees them.

WHAT WE'VE LEARNED ON OUR TRIP TO MARS

Compliant

Positive Characteristics. The compliant person is cooperative in conflict and easy to persuade. She is easy-going and flexible. She is good at collaborative problem solving and easily involves others in decision making. She complies readily with group decisions.

Negative Characteristics. The overly compliant person sometimes simply won't make decisions. He gives in too readily and is too flexible and accommodating. He frustrates a team by agreeing with whomever speaks even when people voice two very opposing points of view. He may need too much direction and structure, and people may not perceive him as a self-starter.

What You Will Get from Them

- Flexibility

- Loyalty

- Collaboration

What You Need to Give Them

- Support for their ideas

- Encouragement

- Structure and procedures to follow

Dominant

Positive Characteristics. The dominant person can be influential in the department or organization. She can have a positive impact and take a strong leadership role. She often has a strong work ethic and commitment to the organization, along with assertiveness and assurance. She can be a strong advocate for taking action and getting the job done.

Negative Characteristics. The overly dominant person is also aggressive and gets angry easily. He may not be very flexible or have much insight into what it takes to collaborate with people. People may tend to perceive him as someone who will act in a somewhat disdainful manner toward other people. He may interrupt other people, monopolize meetings, make a lot of critical comments, and refuse to comply with group decisions even when everyone else agrees. On top of everything else, the dominant person tends to be somewhat intolerant of criticism, so it may be difficult to give him feedback about his behavior.

What You Will Get from Them

- Leadership

- Strong opinions

- Confrontations

What You Need to Give Them

- Opportunities to run things

- Opportunities to compete

- Status symbols

- Opportunities to advance

AFTER OUR TRIP TO MARS

This worksheet will help you think about the concepts presented in this chapter.

1. Which end of the spectrum most characterizes me?

Compliant ← → Dominant

2. How does this trait help me contribute positively to situations?

3. When do I need to "stretch" a bit in the opposite direction?

4. Which end of the spectrum most characterizes those closest to me at work? (If you have chosen to analyze your boss, particular co-workers, and/or employees who are particularly problematic for you at work, continue to analyze that person or persons here.)

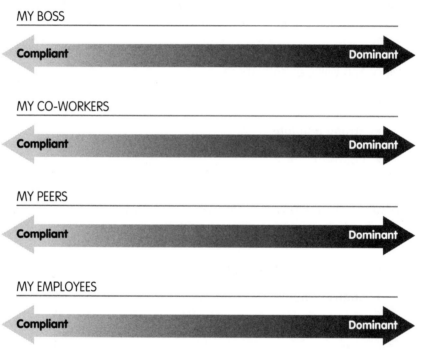

MY BOSS

Compliant ← → Dominant

MY CO-WORKERS

Compliant ← → Dominant

MY PEERS

Compliant ← → Dominant

MY EMPLOYEES

Compliant ← → Dominant

5. How can I best call on these people when I need to use their natural abilities?

6. How can I avoid expecting them to do things that fly in the face of their natural style? How can I stop being disappointed in them or angry at them when they do what just comes naturally to them?

7. How can I change my behavior to get along better with these people?

CHAPTER 7
Employees from Jupiter

Jupiter is the largest of the planets in our solar system and is made up mostly of gasses. It has a "bubbly" spirit, in other words, much like the optimists I am going to talk about in this chapter. Jupiter was also the Roman god of lightning, and you know what pessimists think about the odds of being struck by lightning—they expect it to happen to them on an almost daily basis. Probably the best-known feature of the planet Jupiter is the Great Red Spot, a giant storm that has existed for hundreds of years. What a field day a pessimist could have with that—a storm that never ends!

THE OPTIMIST/THE PESSIMIST

Here's a great example of how an optimist and a pessimist might react in the same situation.

Co-Worker A: "Wow! We won the contract!"

Co-Worker B: "I can't believe we won the contract and now we have all this work to do."

An optimist is *enthusiastic*, generally *happy*, somewhat *naïve*, and *interprets events positively*. He has *high self-esteem* and a *tendency to attribute good intentions to others*.

Pessimists are more *suspicious, serious, realistic,* and somewhat *negative*. They experience more negative life events (because they interpret events negatively). Often they have *low self-esteem*, which they mask with *arrogance*. People need to approach pessimists with understanding and balance, possibly more than with any other personality type. The natural antagonism between optimists and pessimists causes each side to "dig in" and become exaggerated and entrenched in their emotions and behavior. Conflict seems inevitable but can be smoothed with some work and some understanding.

BEFORE WE TRAVEL TO JUPITER

The Big Five personality factor of agreeableness (see the introduction) affects optimism and pessimism a great deal. Emotional intelligence also has a lot to do with it, particularly what Daniel Goleman terms "social deftness" and self-awareness; that is, being able to handle emotions instead of being driven by them.

There is a great deal of research on optimism itself as a *trait* of personality. When I talk about traits, I am talking about something that is a fairly permanent part of someone's style rather than the more fleeting feeling known as a state. For example, if I am feeling optimistic today, that would be a state. If I am an optimistic person most days, that is a trait. The characteristics I am talking about in this book are traits, although any one of them may feel like fleeting states any given day. I may be a very optimistic person in general, but that does not mean that a series of bad days may not leave me feeling pessimistic a time or two in my life.

Which End of the Spectrum Most Characterizes Me?

Do you tend to see the glass as half empty or half full? Do you think other people generally mean well, or are you somewhat suspicious of them? Do you see yourself as the kind of person who makes good choices, whom good things happen to, and who is lucky? Do other people see you as agreeable and cooperative? Or are you a bit more guarded? Do you think it is natural to be competitive with most people; after all, aren't people looking out for themselves? Do you feel like you come up with the "short end of the stick" a lot, that you can't win, or that you have made some bad choices in life?

Which End of the Spectrum Most Characterizes Those Closest to Me at Work: My Boss, My Co-Workers, My Peers, and My Employees?

Look around and see how you might describe those closest to you at work. Then ask yourself: How can you be more accepting of some of the natural reactions of these people? How can you avoid being surprised and irritated when they do things and say things that are, after all, simply their natural style? What kind of responses can you plan that will allow you to better work with them?

I will revisit these questions in the worksheet at the end of the chapter.

JUMPIN' JUPITER: AIN'T IT AWFUL . . . Again!

MegaFoods Market store #428 is getting a new manager! The news began to spread in the usual way employee grapevines spread . . . in ways that are hard to track. By the time the night shift reported for duty at 6 p.m., most employees knew that by Monday morning Ken, the manager for the last six years, would be replaced by someone named Bernadette Balletti. No one had met her, but people were starting to compile the "facts":

- She had been with the company for 10 years.
- She had been a manager for two years.
- She was coming from a district 100 miles north.
- She was married, no children, somewhat young.

Wayne, Dayna, Laurel, and Dan—the night crew—punched in at the time clock and began discussing the new boss as they began the long night of stocking the new grocery load onto the shelves. "I can't believe they're doing this to us," said Wayne. "She's probably some hard charger looking to make a name for herself. I hate breaking in a new boss, especially some young one like this. This is just . . ."

"Wayne, stop," said Dan. "You don't know anything about her. Remember last year, when we had the merger and became MegaFoods? For six months we had to listen to you moan and complain every night about how we were all going to lose our jobs, health benefits, and pensions as soon as the merger came through. I told you then that the difference between you and me was that in six months you were going to have an ulcer and I was going to be fine—and that we were either going to have jobs or we weren't."

"Yeah, well, what if we hate her?"

"And what if we don't? What if we like her just fine?"

"You're just such a Mr. Sunshine."

"And you're a grouch."

It went downhill from there.

JUPITER THE BUBBLY GAS GIANT: CHARACTERISTICS OF AN OPTIMIST

Optimists tend to want to cooperate with people and they like to work in harmony. They value affiliation and getting along with other people. They tend to be helpful and are willing to compromise to get along. They tend to believe in the good intentions of other people and therefore they trust other people. As a result of all of these things, they are fairly likable. They are good-natured and somewhat cheerful most of the time. They're easy to get along with and easy to talk to.

Optimists tend to view the world with a positive outlook. They interpret events positively, so they tend to believe that they are lucky, that things tend to work out for them, and that the world in general is a good place. This, of course, tends to be somewhat of a self-fulfilling prophecy, so good things do tend to happen to them because they interpret things positively. In other words, if they win a cash prize at work, it's a positive thing for them. If pessimists win a cash prize at work, it's a negative thing for them because they have to pay the taxes on it!

Like all of the traits in this book, there are downsides to being an optimist as well. An optimist can be too positive, not see the negatives in a truly negative situation, and thus get blindsided. An optimist can be too trusting, too naïve, and thus be taken advantage of. He may not put enough value on his own priorities to fight for his own point of view hard enough in meetings, negotiations, budget battles, and other corporate wars. He may also avoid conflict and thus see it worsen instead of solving the problems that conflict brings in its wake.

JUPITER THE GOD OF LIGHTNING: CHARACTERISTICS OF A PESSIMIST

Pessimists are serious, suspicious, somewhat negative people. They aren't necessarily antagonistic toward other people; they just don't put a lot of value in being cooperative. In fact, they may be the ones who are needed in a situation to point out the danger to an overly cooperative, naïve optimist. Pessimists may be skeptical of other people's motives and are unlikely to be overly trusting of other people. This may cause them to come across as being suspicious or unfriendly. In extreme cases, people may see them as antagonistic or uncooperative.

In the workplace, pessimists are good at being analytical, focusing on the task, and focusing on the outcome. They are not sidetracked by concerns about how people are feeling or anxiety about hurting other people's feelings. In business dealings, they can often see the hidden motives of con artists who may be good at fooling the optimists.

JOVIAN COMBINATIONS

And now let's look at how the types combine at work: two optimists, two pessimists, and one of each type.

Two Optimists

As you might expect, two optimists get along just fine in the workplace. They may have no conflicts, but they may not be very productive either. This is due to their overly agreeable nature. For an extremely agreeable person who avoids conflict, it is hard to correct a fellow employee. So he may see someone doing a job all wrong and just let it go on. Or he might see a lot of problems with a suggestion someone might make in a meeting but will say, "Gee, that could work, I guess . . ." because he is afraid of hurting the person's feelings.

Two optimists may also have a difficult time making a decision because they want to give in to the other. Again, this is due to their overly agreeable nature. Imagine two optimists approaching a doorway. The conversation might go something like this.

"Please, after you!"

"Oh, no, you first."

"I insist . . ."

If it takes them 10 minutes to get through a doorway, imagine how long it might take them to make an important decision. Two problems exist here. The optimists may see only the good in the proposal or task, or their agreeable natures cause them to want to agree with what their colleagues suggest. This can be very dangerous and blind them to land mines in the proposal or course of action. Here, more than ever, the team needs balance. And let us remind ourselves of the fact that this balance requires us to overcome the very natural annoyance that comes when optimists work with pessimists.

Two Pessimists

Two pessimists actually get along pretty well when working together. They agree on the major issues, which is that the outlook for everything is pretty gloomy. They can bring each other down even further, of course, but that may have a paradoxical cheering effect on them, because it validates their view of the world.

If assigned to a task force or project, however, chances are the project will be (if they have this power) cancelled. The pessimists will enthusiastically compile all the reasons it will never work and may even present them in a forceful, analytical, well-organized manner.

One of Each

It is important to have both pessimists and optimists in meetings, task forces, and business deals. It is equally as important that each side understands and appreciates what the other has to offer. As we saw in the case of Dan and Wayne on the night crew in the opening case study, the two quickly irritate each other with their very different views of the world.

So how can optimists and pessimists be of value to each other? That is the tricky part. A lot depends on where you are in the scheme of things. If you are a boss, you need to make people appreciate the differences and manage the inevitable conflicts well. If you are not a boss, you need to do what you can to manage your relationships with your co-workers. And what if the problem *is* your boss? Well, there are some things you can do there, too.

Co-Workers. If you are an optimist with a pessimist co-worker (or a pessimist with an optimist co-worker), there is one very important thing that you need to keep reminding yourself: You are not going to change your co-worker's personality. Personality traits may be at least 50 percent inborn, and the rest are pretty set in stone by the time we reach grade-school age. Barring any catastrophic illness or traumatic life event, our personalities simply don't change in any bedrock kind of way after we become adults. (Our behavior—our habits—may change, but our personality by definition is made up of the fairly stable and unchanging characteristics that define us.) A type-A hardcharger may change a bit if he survives his first heart attack, and someone who survives being a prisoner of war for seven years may come back changed by that ordeal, but for the average person in today's average workplace, we can rule out any basic personality changes.

So let's get the frustration and wasted time out of the way right off the top. Quit trying to talk the person out of being a pessimist. Facts, figures, and logic about why the world is a positive place are not only not going to change her mind, they are going to (1) annoy her, and (2) convince her you are an unrealistic, naïve individual who shouldn't be out on the streets alone. (The same advice, remember, applies to the pessimist trying to talk someone out of being an optimist.)

What do you do? Accept her view of the world and move on. Begin with agreement and use "us" and "we." Create a partnership with the other person. Say something like, "Yes, the world might end tomorrow. Just in case it doesn't, let's get these files completed." And say it in a calm, cheerful, professional tone of voice, with no eye rolling or heavy sighs.

Do your homework. Know what the pessimist tends to say and be prepared to respond. For the one who tends to say, "This will never work, we tried that before," say, "Yes, I know we have tried it this way before. I would disagree that it has never worked. I can think of at least twice that it has worked very well. Last March we sold 8,000 copies and made a nice profit, and before that it worked very well in our Northeast division."

If you are pessimist with an optimist co-worker, the same advice applies. Think of the frustration and wasted time you will save as soon as you stop trying to get that person to change. Instead, bring him down gently. Begin with agreement and use "we." Say something like, "Yes, the salesperson from Widget-World seemed like a very nice person, and we did enjoy the doughnuts. I still think it is important we look over the figures very carefully. Remember when we agreed to that contract last year and were cheated out of $2,000?" I know you really want to say, "*You* agreed to that contract and *you* caused us to lose $2,000." Resist. You are a team here. The person you are talking to knows who caused the problem last year. Don't rub it in.

Boss and Employee. At first it may seem that working for agreeable, optimistic bosses would be wonderful. After a while though, it can be frustrating. In Chapter 1 I talked about the Job Characteristics Model of job satisfaction and noted that one of the things we need to be satisfied on the job is feedback. Feedback includes knowing both what is going well in our work as well as what is not going well—constructive criticism. We need feedback to know how we can improve on the job. Very agreeable bosses may have a hard time giving their employees constructive criticism.

First of all, if you are one of these bosses, you probably know it already because you hate giving annual performance reviews. Your boss has told you that you can't just give everyone "excellent" or whatever your company's top measure is. So you go in to the review feeling bad about giving anyone any kind of constructive criticism. Even on a day-to-day basis, when you see an employee doing something you know she shouldn't be doing, you prefer to avoid the confrontation and walk by it as if you hadn't seen it.

If you've been a manager for any time at all, you know you can't continue to be this way, so you've probably learned some behaviors that allowed you to survive. You have to confront unacceptable employee behavior. And you can do it in a non-confrontational, nondefensive way. Optimistic, agreeable people need a lot of training in coaching and counseling. These are gentle management techniques that are actually helpful to employees because they tell employees what is required on the job. Agreeable managers can feel that they are doing their jobs without being disagreeable.

If you work for one of these bosses, think about how you want to approach her. Simply asking for feedback may get her usual reply of, "Oh, everything is fine." You may have to learn how to ask for specifics and be very careful not to act defensive or make excuses. If she does make a remark that is the least bit critical, thank her. Let her know that criticism is welcomed.

Employee and Boss. The case of an optimistic employee working for a pessimistic boss is much more difficult. Remember, in the case of a pessimistic boss I am talking about a person who, although realistic, takes a somewhat suspicious view of the world and people in general. Clearly one of the things an employee must do in this case is work to earn that person's trust over time. And this does not happen quickly.

If you are that pessimistic boss, remember that people do need to hear positives once in a while. Even if you have to write yourself a script and memorize it like a stage actor, begin your conversations with your employees with what they did well. Then you can tell them the bad news.

You probably know whether you work for an optimist or a pessimist. And like everything I am talking about and will remind you of again and again, none of these characteristics are all bad. The pessimist can be a great businessperson. He can be analytical, realistic, and have a great head for business deals. He may not be the warmest, friendliest boss in the world. If you can deal with that, you may survive. One thing to try that works with some of these bosses is a touch of humor, carefully applied. I had a boss like this once, and occasionally in the midst of one of his tirades, I would ask with a smile ". . . and what were the merits of what I did?" Or in a staff meeting, when he was tearing apart a report that the staff had put together, I would turn to the others and say, "What he meant to say was, 'Thanks for the overtime you put in yesterday to put this report together.'" Again, it was always done with a smile and a bit of humor.

HOW TO BE MORE BALANCED IF YOU'RE AN OPTIMIST

It's hard to tell an optimist to be less agreeable. But optimism can be taken to an extreme. Optimists need to recognize when their agreeableness is getting in the way. Is there too much collaboration going on when a decision needs to be made? If the decision really isn't that important, just decide and move on. If the decision is important, enlist the aid of some decision-making tools or a pessimist or two who can be more analytical and less concerned with collaboration and people's feelings.

Optimists also need to be aware of times when the intentions of others around them are not necessarily honorable. Sometimes the pessimists around you are correct. When signing contracts, making business deals, or entering into negotiations, if you know that you are on the highly agreeable side, you may want to enlist the aid of someone who is more balanced or even on the pessimistic side.

If you are an optimistic co-worker, understand that you might annoy your fellow co-workers with your constantly positive attitude. I know this can be hard to understand, but sometimes, especially during stressful times, it pays to tone it down a little. It also helps if you empathize with the stress others seem to be feeling. Listen to the things you are in the habit of saying as well. Vary those a little bit. If you constantly say things like, "That's right!" "True!" "You're right," or "I agree," that can get old. Try something different. Perhaps you could try asking people more about what they just said—something like, "Interesting. Tell me more about that."

If you are a boss, you probably already know that you can't simply be agreeable all the time. You have to coach your employees, you have to let them know when they're not doing their jobs, and you may even have to fire people. Highly agreeable bosses sometimes don't continue as managers, because they simply can't handle doing these things. If you are reasonably high in the agreeable characteristic and can learn to do these things in a calm, professional manner, you can be an excellent boss.

As an employee, how do you relate to your pessimist boss better if you are an optimist? Keep in mind that your boss needs to hear the bad news as well as the good. It is particularly hard to disagree with your boss. When the boss throws out an idea in a meeting and says, "What do you all think?" an agreeable person finds it particularly hard to say, "That's a terrible idea." Time, trust, and your relationship with your boss will make this easier to do. Practice ways to say, "Yes, we could do that. Have we thought about what would happen if . . . ?" and then state your concerns. Practice those kinds of communication methods, and you can continue to be agreeable but still helpful to your boss. Think of it as being helpful instead of being disagreeable.

HOW TO BE MORE BALANCED IF YOU'RE A PESSIMIST

Pessimists need to recognize when their lack of agreeableness is getting in the way. Sometimes a negotiation, business deal, or contract will go much more smoothly with a bit of agreeableness thrown into the mix. Sometimes people really do have good intentions. Sometimes a bit of people skills can cause the negotiation to go your way. If this does not come naturally to you, you may want to enlist the aid of someone in your organization or on your team who you know is agreeable. Hint: This is liable to be an annoying, perennially cheerful, upbeat, naïve individual whom you don't like to be teamed with.

Sometimes it helps just to draw back a bit yourself. Practice the social chitchat before going in to a meeting. Decide ahead of time which point you are willing to give in on. Understand that in order to get what you want, you're going to give up a couple of things in return.

As a co-worker, you have a lot to offer your fellow co-workers, but you probably have a reputation of being a bit difficult to work with. You may consider this reputation undeserved and may even resent it. You can work with it. You need to use the "yes, and" method that I've talked about in this chapter. You also need to use "we." Think about the fact that you may have a reputation of disagreeing with most of what is brought forth in meetings. This may take a while to change. But you do have a lot to offer, and you need to get that heard. So when someone brings up something you disagree with, you need to begin with agreement, strange as that may sound. "Yes, that sounds interesting. And here's something else to consider: We may need to . . ." That person is listening to you now in a nondefensive way because you started a conversation in an optimistic, upbeat fashion. It's a start.

As a boss, you have a lot to offer, but it may be overlooked due to your overall reputation as a somewhat pessimistic individual. Employees may see you as someone who doesn't offer them a lot of positive comments. I know you might say, "They get paid, what else do they want?" Well, we know from the Job Characteristics Model that they need a lot more, including positive feedback, to be motivated to do their best work. We also know about the self-fulfilling prophecy, which tells us that if you expect the worst out of people, that's what you will get. So if you think your employees have bad intentions, you'll tend to get that from them. Really look at your employees, talk to them, and find out whom you can trust, what their intentions are, and whom you've got working for you. Script your conversations if you have to, but start off with the positives. As I said in the above paragraph, start with "yes" not "no," and "and" not "but."

For instance, consider this terrible comment from a boss: "Bad idea. It'll never fly. I'd never take that to the big bosses anyway, not during budget week."

Now consider this good comment from a boss: "Yes, that's interesting. And I can see that you have put a lot of work into it. Thanks. Let's get together this week and go over it in more detail, because this is budget week, the big bosses are tied up, and I couldn't take it to them yet anyway. I can see a couple of places that are going to need a little bit work before we could submit it."

As an employee, keep in mind that your boss has probably heard a lot of pessimism from you already and may be tired of it. Like those in the other categories, you may feel you have an undeserved reputation. All you're trying to do is be realistic and tell the truth, and you may feel surrounded by a bunch of naïve people with their heads buried in the sand. Be that as it may, it may make your life easier if you could be a bit more balanced. How are you going to approach your boss more effectively? You will do that by using some of the same methods that I've been talking about already. Watch your habits of speech. What tends to be the first thing out of your mouth? Change it. Practice what you're going to say next time and write it out if you have to. Pretend you're an actor on a stage and learn your lines. Say "yes" instead of "no." Say "interesting" to buy yourself some time to think.

 ## WHAT WE'VE LEARNED ON OUR TRIP TO JUPITER

Optimists

Positive Characteristics. Optimists have a real trust in other people. They value cooperation and collaboration. They tend to believe in the goodness of other people and are likable and good-natured. They have a positive outlook on life.

Negative Characteristics. Optimists may view the world a little too positively; that is, they don't see the negatives even when they need to. They may trust people who don't deserve to be trusted. When they are loyal to someone, that person may take advantage of them. When they hold an opinion that is unpopular, even when that opinion may be correct, they are willing to give it up. They may be taken advantage of.

What You Will Get from Them

- Loyalty
- A positive outlook

- Agreeableness

- Enthusiasm

What You Need to Give Them

- A positive environment to work in

- Criticism that is always constructive

- Feedback that is tempered with realism

Pessimists

Positive Characteristics. Pessimists are serious about their work and realistic in their outlook. They tend to be focused on the task at work and driven to achieve their outcomes. They can be very independent.

Negative Characteristics. Pessimists are somewhat suspicious of other people. They tend to take a negative view of life and most life events. As a result, they are somewhat skeptical of and competitive with other people. They may come across as arrogant and unfriendly.

What You Will Get from Them

- Worst-case scenarios

- Cynicism

- Realism

What You Need to Give Them

- Appreciation of their contributions

- Feedback on the value of what they have offered

- Teammates who can ignore the negative emotion

AFTER OUR TRIP TO JUPITER

This worksheet will help you think about the concepts presented in this chapter.

1. Which end of the spectrum most characterizes me?

2. How does this trait help me contribute positively to situations?

3. When do I need to "stretch" a bit in the opposite direction?

4. Which end of the spectrum most characterizes those closest to me at work? (If you have chosen to analyze your boss, particular co-workers, and/or employees who are particularly problematic for you at work, continue to analyze that person or persons here.)

MY BOSS

MY CO-WORKERS

MY PEERS

MY EMPLOYEES

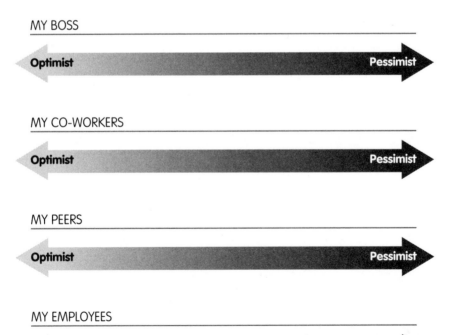

5. How can I best call on these people when I need to use their natural abilities?

6. How can I avoid expecting them to do things that fly in the face of their natural style? How can I stop being disappointed in them or angry at them when they do what just comes naturally to them?

7. How can I change my behavior to get along better with these people?

CHAPTER 8
Saturn Is So Different

Saturn, with its distinctive rings, is the most different looking of all of the planets. Galileo noticed its odd appearance as long ago as 1610 and was bothered by it, much as the people I am going to talk about in this chapter bother one another. The trait I will associate with the planet Saturn has to do with liking the tried-and-true in life versus always wondering what is new and exciting. In others words, some people stick to the status quo and some try something quite different, like wearing a set of prominent rings in order to stand out from the crowd.

THE CONFORMIST/THE EXPERIMENTER

Do you and your co-workers ever have conversations like this?

"Want to go out for lunch today?"

"Sure. Want to try that new Italian place on the corner?"

"Oh, no. How about Gino's?"

"We eat Gino's food at least twice a week. Aren't you tired of it?"

Conformists are *conscientious, conventional, conservative, orga-*

nized, and *hardworking*. They like to plan their work and work their plan. Experimenters are *expedient*, like to *try new ways*, are *adventuresome*, and *value autonomy*. Organizations benefit from having both of these types around—as long as they can manage to keep them from each others' throats.

BEFORE WE TRAVEL TO SATURN

Conformists and experimenters are two types of people who are at the ends of a spectrum related to another of the Big Five personality characteristics: conscientiousness (see the introduction). They are also related to how we react to change, how flexible we are, and how much freedom and autonomy we value. In the Jungian temperament types I talked about in the introduction, there is a clear connection between these two types and the difference between what is called judging and perceiving. Judgers prefer a more structured lifestyle and perceivers are more flexible and adaptable.

Which End of the Spectrum Most Characterizes Me?

Do you like to stick with what you know? When planning an annual event such as a budget meeting, a holiday party, or a strategy session, is your first move to bring out last year's notes and see what you need to adjust to make it work for this year? Do you see a lot of value in sticking with what has worked in the past? Or do you like to break new ground and try new things, even if that increases the risk of failure?

Which End of the Spectrum Most Characterizes Those Closest to Me at Work: My Boss, My Co-Workers, My Peers, and My Employees?

If you work closely with people who are the opposite of you on this trait, chances are they either make you very nervous or cause you great annoyance. You can already guess which way it goes; if you are a conformist surrounded by experimenters, you might feel very uneasy, and if you are an experimenter surrounded by conformists, you might feel stifled and tied down.

SATURNIANS AT WORK: CONSCIENTIOUS OR OBSESSIVE?

The student services department at State University was getting ready for another new-student orientation. It expected more than 200 freshmen, and the 110-page handouts introducing them to every aspect of campus life needed to get to the campus print shop. Jake, the head of student services, was not really surprised that the handouts were not ready yet. He knew that the employee in charge of the orientation, Luis, was a bit of a perfectionist and tended to obsess over every last detail. That meant that things tended to get done at the last minute, but Jake had gotten used to the fact that Luis did get things done eventually, as long as he was given a definite deadline. He just never got things done early!

As Jake walked by Luis's desk, he saw the master copy of the handout opened up and Luis laboring over it with what looked like a felt-tipped pen. "What are you doing?" he asked. Luis did not look up, but replied, "The new word processing program prints out bulleted lists in the form of circles, not bullets."

- ○ New handouts
- ○ Bullet lists
- ○ Looked like
- ○ This

Luis was filling in the circles by hand so they looked just like the old handouts.

- ● Old handouts
- ● Bullet lists
- ● Looked like
- ● This

Jake leaned over and saw what he meant. "Luis, is this really a big deal? The students won't notice any difference."

"They are supposed to be bullets. They look better that way."

"You really could be working more productively on other

things or even going home! It's almost quitting time, and these have to get to the print shop."

"Well, I can't quit in the middle of the handout and have the first half be solid bullets and the second half be circles! I was just trying to be sure that the things going out of our office were of top quality and consistent."

Of course, Jake and Luis had held conversations like this one before. Jake was frustrated because it was often hard to argue with Luis's logic, yet at times like this Jake knew that Luis was just wasting time. Luis always pulled the old "quality" argument yet sometimes worked until midnight before a project was due in order to have it completed and only reluctantly turned it in then. When Jake insisted that "good enough was good enough," Luis made it clear (without saying it in so many words) that he felt some people in the department were allowed to get away with shoddy work. As a boss, Jake felt his hands were tied. How do you discipline an employee for staying late, working hard, and being a perfectionist?

PLAIN-VANILLA PLANET: CHARACTERISTICS OF A CONFORMIST

Conformists are conscientious, conventional, and can be somewhat timid. They are orderly, organized, practical, and hard-working. They are conservative in their outlook on things and very thorough in their approach to tasks. They have a strong sense of duty, so they feel responsible and they follow the rules. They like to know what the rules are and they feel somewhat anxious in a situation where anything goes.

Conformists like to "plan the work and work the plan." They generally do not require a lot of supervision, because they are fairly self-disciplined as long as the task is well-defined. Once given a task, they tend to be very persistent and they will keep at it even in the face of boredom.

Scratch the surface of a conformist and you find a perfectionist. Take this perfectionism a little too far and you'll find a person who is overly self-critical, who cannot see the benefit of new ways of doing things, and who is very fond of the standard operating procedures. Conformists put so much value in competence—their own and others'—that people can rarely convince them of the worth of trying something new. That, after all, means giving up that highly valued competence in the old way of doing things. Conformists take a great deal of pleasure in their achievements, and their achievements come from doing things they already know how to do well. Because conformists like to have things organized, planned, and settled, they can feel a great deal of anxiety when they have to do things a different way. This is one of the reasons there is such conflict when conformists have to work with experimenters.

SATURN'S REMARKABLE RINGS: CHARACTERISTICS OF AN EXPERIMENTER

Experimenters are creative, flexible, and like new ways of doing things. At work, they value autonomy and dislike close supervision and tasks that are strictly defined. Although conformists find rules and structure comforting, experimenters see rules as limiting and stifling. Experimenters like to keep their options open. Their philosophy is that you never know what might happen in a given day. So why make up rules that are simply going to limit the options? Although rules and structure give conformists a sense of control, it is keeping their options open that give experimenters a sense of control.

Experimenters tend to have a strong sense of curiosity. They like to expand their knowledge, which, more than the conformist, they acknowledge as being incomplete. So in a meeting they tend to want to put off making a decision and gather more information, but the conformists push for a decision. Of course, in a work situation, this may cause people to see experimenters as indecisive, although experimenters see themselves as flexible and spontaneous. Making a decision quickly sometimes feels to the experimenter like a trap. It cuts him off from other, possibly smarter, decisions. His sense of achievement comes from doing something creative and new; he wonders where the achievement is in simply following someone else's rules to complete a task.

In a strategy session, planning meeting, or even when just planning the next holiday party, the experimenters are the ones who want to start from scratch. They will find it boring when the conformists pull out last year's file and simply want to adjust what they did last year. "Let's do something completely different," is the catchphrase of the experimenter. If the experimenters get their way, the company may experience something completely different and may get fabulous results or a spectacular failure. That doesn't have far-reaching implications if it's the holiday party, but if it's the five-year strategic plan, it can affect the survival of the organization. I worked with one organization in which a group of experimenters wanted to do something besides the "hotel ballroom/beef-chicken-fish/boring raffle" holiday party. They arranged for a cocktail and hors d'oeuvres tour of a local design center. It was generally deemed a disaster. There wasn't enough food, there was nowhere to sit, the tours were boring, and most people drove through local fast food outlets to get something to eat on the way home.

SATURN'S COMBINATIONS

How do two conformists work together? Two experimenters? One of each? Let's take a look.

Two Conformists

Two conformists will get along just fine. They will approach a task with the same level of practicality and planning. They agree with each others' work ethic and think that the other person has the right attitude toward the job. They may not be very creative or do anything out of the ordinary, but they will get the job done and it will be done with all the details taken care of.

Two or more conformists will be best at jobs that have clear parameters and clear guidelines. They may not be good at jobs where they are asked to brainstorm, be creative, or are left to their own devices. They may not work well in start-up organizations, where the rules are not even established yet, the strategies are fluid, or the rules change daily.

Two Experimenters

Two experimenters will work together well also. They will be creative, have fun, and get the job done, although it may be in ways that no one expected. They may also have a bit too much fun; the task may develop in ways such that it is unrecognizable by the time it is completed. You may have to remind a task force of experimenters to refer to the ultimate goals and objectives of a project throughout the project timeline so that they do not range too far from the original intent.

A pair or a team of experimenters will sometimes let some small details fall between the cracks. Their finished product may have some rough edges, but it will get done. Experimenters do very well in start-up organizations, as entrepreneurs, or in situations where they are asked to brainstorm or use their own judgment.

One of Each

A mixture of the two types can be an explosive situation. As in all of our examples, the critical component is to understand whom you are dealing with. As I said, the conformist finds it comforting to follow the rules, to work to a detailed plan, and to work within a structure. It arouses quite a bit of anxiety to break those rules.

Conversely, an experimenter finds it comforting to have no rules, to work with very little structure, and to find new ways to do things. He finds it annoying and restrictive to work to a detailed plan. Clearly, simply throwing two of these people together is a situation ripe for conflict. But, as we showed, it can also be quite helpful to have one of each on a team because they can hold each others' negative characteristics in check. This can only happen if they understand and appreciate what the other is doing, however.

Co-Workers. When two co-workers find themselves assigned to a task, and one is an experimenter and one is a conformist, they can find the going very tough. The nature of the problem depends on the nature of the task. If they are on a planning committee, they may have difficulty reaching a decision for the reasons that I talked about in the "One of Each" section. The conformist wants to go with the tried and true, and the experimenter wants to try something different. If they are asked to work on a task force (not planning a task, but working on one that has already been decided upon), they have problems because the way they approach the task is very different. You can often diagnose this situation because there are accusations of sloppiness on one side and obsessiveness on the other.

Because the co-worker relationship is essentially that of equals or peers, neither may have the power to force his or her will onto the situation. In this case, the pair or the team may have to ask the boss for intervention or guidance. In the case of a planning meeting, the majority may rule or the meeting facilitator may simply have to use his own facilitation skills. In the case of the task force, going to the boss and asking for her intervention might be helpful. What generally happens over time is that co-workers get to know one another's style and (one hopes) appreciate it.

It would be helpful if the team could work together effectively by allowing the experimenters time to brainstorm and come up with new and interesting ways to perform the task. Let them be creative. The conformists can take notes, contain their anxiety, and allow some agenda time for this to happen. Then the conformists can fill in the details, blend in the new and interesting ways in such a manner that the job still gets done, and still accomplish the main objectives. This does require time and trust, and it generally happens after a team has been together for a while.

Boss and Employee. In the case of the conformist boss who has experimenter employees, obviously the boss has some power to set the tone for the organization or the department. With this trait, perhaps more than the others, the boss's style dictates the policies and procedures. A conformist boss is going to be conservative, is going to be careful, and is going to have a tendency to go with the tried and true.

How is an experimenter employee going to handle this? The obvious answer is simply to realize that the boss is the boss and to live with it. The more subtle answer is that you can begin slowly to make some inroads if you are careful. Keep in mind that the more new and exciting the recommendation or suggestion is, the more anxiety you're going to arouse in your boss. Begin with small suggestions, and tie them to what you have already done in the past. The closer you can get to the tried and true, the more comforting that will be to the boss. Think of yourself as a salesperson: You want to get the boss to say yes, so you make small suggestions first.

Consider Susan. Her office staff members hated everything about their weekly meetings. They met in her office, gave one-by-one updates about their areas, took turns taking minutes, then distributed those minutes later that day. The office was small and they felt cramped. Susan sat behind her desk and they lined up in a row facing her. They had no opportunity for any exchange of information or conversation. Taking the minutes, typing them up, and distributing them took a great deal of time and felt redundant. Yet Susan immediately rejected every suggestion for change. So with the help of a consultant from their internal organizational-development department, they came up with an eight-week plan.

The first week, one of the employees asked if he could pull the chairs into a circle so that people could see one another while they spoke. Susan seemed a little uneasy, but there didn't seem to be a good reason to say no to the suggestion. At the end of the meeting, they all thanked her very warmly for allowing the change and gave her specific feedback that being allowed to see one another and speak to one another during the meeting was very helpful to them as a group.

At the end of the next meeting, they remarked that because the circle of chairs was so effective, it might even be more effective if they arranged to meet in one of the conference rooms instead. One of the staff volunteered to see if a conference room was available each Monday morning for their meetings. Again, because it was a small change built on the change they had already made, Susan agreed.

At the end of the next meeting, one of the staff members asked the other staff members if they ever used the minutes of the meetings that were distributed. They unanimously said that they did not, because each person brought handouts to accompany their verbal briefings. A second staff member then asked Susan, "I'm wondering if it would save us some productive work time if we were able to quit taking minutes and distributing them. We are all here and able to hear what is being discussed, and we get the handouts. Would it be possible to dispense with the taking of minutes?" Again, this was presented as a logical change and it was handled well, and Susan agreed. And if she had not, oh well, at least they had made some inroads. They would keep trying. At the end of their carefully planned eight-week program, the meetings had changed a great deal for the better, but they would not have made those inroads had they not taken Susan's style as a conformist into account.

Employee and Boss. The experimenter boss who has conformist employees is in a different situation. In this case, the boss is not entirely in charge of the policies and procedures, unless of course he is the owner of the organization. A lot depends on the organizational culture. An organization may be either conservative or more risk-taking. How widely an experimenter is able to use his style depends on his place in the organization; is he the CEO, a manager, or a supervisor? Does he have the ability to make policy for the organization or is he simply in the position of carrying it out? In any case, with an experimenter we have a boss who is somewhat freewheeling, who wants to do things differently, and who is flexible, open to change, and somewhat casual. And if he has conformist employees, they like structure, they like plans, and they don't like to just wing it.

This set of circumstances very likely frustrates a conformist employee. He may go back to the boss several times looking for more direction on a task. There is a great deal of room for misunderstanding here. Remember, the conformist is not an employee who needs a great deal of supervision. He simply likes to know what is required of him in a task. Once he knows, he will do it and do it well. But an experimenter boss is likely to misunderstand him as someone who is needy and demanding. The boss may tell him, "Use your best judgment." But that is really not enough direction for a conformist if he is new to the task. He needs to be given a direction to go in. He is wondering, "Whom can I ask? What did we do last year? Point me in the right direction and I will do this task and do it well."

Remember the case of Jake and Luis in the opening example of this chapter? Jake has to be careful what tasks he assigns Luis. Luis is excellent at well-defined tasks and does not do so well at ambiguous, creative tasks. Jake also has to make sure that Luis understands and appreciates deadlines, and he has to make sure that he doesn't praise Luis for things like working overtime. Previous bosses had praised Luis for working until midnight the night before a new-student orientation. Jake should tell Luis that if he is here until midnight, he has not prepared himself well and needs to do the job within the allotted time.

So if you are a conformist employee with an experimenter boss, how do you handle that situation? It seems that you would be in a constant state of anxiety. Once you realize you're in this situation, it might be time to sit down with the boss and have a negotiation session. Explain that you do not want to come across as needy or clinging, that you actually are a very good employee, but that you do need a little more direction. Say something like, "Can we possibly start off the task with some structure?" If the boss can't tell you exactly what it is he does want, can he point you to some resources that can make the task clearer? Sometimes, frankly, this relationship does just doesn't work out very well. Sometimes conformists have to find someone else in the organization—a co-worker, someone from another department, or even the boss's boss—who can give them the direction they need.

HOW TO BE MORE BALANCED IF YOU'RE A CONFORMIST

How do you know if you're a conformist? Generally, you can tell because you feel anxious when deadlines approach and your work doesn't feel quite perfect. You also like to do things the way you have always done them, and you get nervous when people are always trying to suggest new ways of doing things.

As a co-worker, use that anxiety as a cue to yourself that it may be time to relax and think about the positive aspects of what someone else is recommending. Think before you speak. Challenge yourself to say one positive thing about whatever it is the person is suggesting. Then feel free to bring up your concerns. You can even ask the experimenter to return the favor: Ask him if he sees any merits to what your concerns are.

If you are a conformist who verges on being a perfectionist, challenge yourself to recognize when good enough is good enough. I know, we're talking about the habits of a lifetime here, but remind yourself that not everything has to be perfect.

In fact, find a small project that doesn't matter so much and allow yourself to do it in an imperfect way. Yes, it will feel funny, and it will make you feel anxious, but that's the point. You are practicing to be more balanced.

If you are a conformist and a boss, you may be more like Susan than you know. When employees make suggestions, you may have very good and logical reasons why they will never work, but stop and think a moment. Listen to your employees' suggestions. Ask for more information. Ask them to do a little more research and tell you more about the ramifications of their ideas. Tell them, if possible, that you would like to do a pilot test of their ideas and see how they work. You may all learn something.

As an employee, remember that your boss isn't trying to annoy you when she gives you a task that seems very vague. She may indeed be trying to get you to use your best judgment. So why don't you try to do the research yourself, find the resources you need, and do the job the way you think it should be done best? That way, you don't get the reputation of being needy, you don't annoy the boss, and you still get the job done efficiently and effectively the way you'd like to get it done.

HOW TO BE MORE BALANCED IF YOU'RE AN EXPERIMENTER

Conformists just love to rain on your parade, don't they? You go in to the meeting very excited about all of your new ideas for this year's strategy session, only to be met with blank stares. You start to hear the usual hackneyed phrases like, "But we've never done it that way." As they begin to pull out their yellowed note cards from five years ago, you sink back into your chair and think, "Here we go again." As an experimenter, your life as a co-worker can be frustrating. Your enthusiasm for new ideas causes you to run into brick walls. Paradoxically, the only way to really get your new ideas heard is to rein in your enthusiasm. You scare these people. You have to come in slowly, present your ideas a little at a time, and as Susan's employees did in the example, treat it as a long-term plan that exposes an idea a little bit at a time in small steps.

As an experimenter boss, just remember that your employees

need more from you than you might expect, and it is not because they are bad employees. In fact, they are very good employees! They are just different from you. Don't be disappointed when you have a great new idea and they welcome it with less than enthusiasm. They may like to do the same things over and over; don't assume that just because you would be bored with the same old routine that they are as well. A boss I know was always surprised when he would plan a "treat" for his employees in the way of new equipment, different procedures, or a change in traditions only to find out every time that they were disappointed. ("But we always have our holiday party at the Downtown Inn!") He was thinking of what he would like, not what they would like.

Involve your employees in any needed changes. Ask them what they would prefer. If the change is inevitable (mandated by corporate, for example), enlist their help in how the department is going to get it done. Lay out the "what" for them and let them help plan the "how." Avoid change for the sake of change; I know you find that exhilarating, but perhaps you can find that thrill in your peer group or at home.

If you are an experimenter employee, everything I have said thus far applies to you as well. Take your lesson from Susan's team. Suggest small, easy changes and praise your boss when she makes them. Suggest changes based on logic and point out the logical benefits once again when the boss makes the changes. If the boss says no, accept it gracefully and move on. If worst comes to worst, you may need to think about your fit with your organization. Some organizations are flexible, risk-taking, and innovative, and you may want to find one that is a good fit with your personality.

 ## WHAT WE'VE LEARNED ON OUR TRIP TO SATURN

Conformist

Positive Characteristics. A conformist is a conscientious, conventional, conservative, organized, practical person. She is thorough and hardworking. She tends to be a bit cautious, has a sense of duty, and follows the rules. She is careful and responsible, and she likes to plan the work and work the plan. She is self-disciplined and persistent.

Negative Characteristics. A conformist can also be somewhat timid. He has a tendency to resist change and can become a perfectionist. Because of the perfectionist tendency, he can take a long time to complete a task and can be very self-critical. Conformists are not necessarily very creative and may not do well at ambiguous tasks.

What You Will Get from Them

- Persistence
- Task-orientation
- Detail-orientation

What You Need to Give Them

- Deadlines that don't change without warning
- Well-defined tasks
- The comfort of the familiar

Experimenter

Positive Characteristics. An experimenter is expedient, likes to experiment with new ways, and is adventuresome. He is creative and values autonomy.

Negative Characteristics. Experimenters can be a bit sloppy with repetitive tasks. They may resist just on general principles if forced to do something according to standard operating procedures.

What You Will Get from Them

- Flexibility
- New ideas and possibilities
- Creativity

What You Need to Give Them

- Flexible schedules
- Autonomy
- Task variety

AFTER OUR TRIP TO SATURN

This worksheet will help you think about the concepts presented in this chapter.

1. Which end of the spectrum most characterizes me?

Conformist ←————————————————————→ Experimenter

2. How does this trait help me contribute positively to situations?

3. When do I need to "stretch" a bit in the opposite direction?

4. Which end of the spectrum most characterizes those closest to me at work? (If you have chosen to analyze your boss, particular co-workers, and/or employees who are particularly problematic for you at work, continue to analyze that person or persons here.)

MY BOSS _____

Conformist ←————————————————————→ Experimenter

MY CO-WORKERS

Conformist ← → **Experimenter**

MY PEERS

Conformist ← → **Experimenter**

MY EMPLOYEES

Conformist ← → **Experimenter**

5. How can I best call on these people when I need to use their natural abilities?

6. How can I avoid expecting them to do things that fly in the face of their natural style? How can I stop being disappointed in them or angry at them when they do what just comes naturally to them?

7. How can I change my behavior to get along better with these people?

CHAPTER 9
The Boss from Uranus

Named for the ancient Greek god of the heavens, Uranus was the first planet discovered in modern times through the use of a telescope. The six planets from Mercury out to Saturn are all visible to the naked eye and therefore were known from ancient times. (Uranus had been spotted many times, too, but was thought to be a star.) Uranus has a very thick cloud cover and an atmosphere with very few features. It has liquid rock at the core and is covered by an ocean. It is thus a very straightforward planet, which I will use to exemplify very straightforward personality traits.

THE TRUE FRIEND/THE DIPLOMAT

How do you tell someone that his fly is unzipped? Maybe you take the direct approach, telling him to "zip up!" Or maybe you feel that the best approach is to pretend you never saw it and spare him embarrassment. Which is the best way? Is there a best way, or does it depend upon the circumstances?

There is a personality factor that influences how you communicate with people. At one end of the spectrum you will find the very *direct, open,* and *honest* person. At the other end is the *tactful, diplomatic* soul. Either person can be very useful to you, or very annoying. It really depends on the circumstances, doesn't it? The tactful, diplomatic person who ignores your open fly may annoy you because she allowed you to shake hands with the CEO without alerting you to your grooming mishap. The person who takes the direct approach may embarrass you in front of other people.

For the purposes of this chapter, I will call the ends of the spectrum on this trait the true friend and the diplomat. Only a true friend will tell you when you have toilet paper sticking to your shoe, that your new hairstyle looks terrible on you, or that your idea for a new project is truly a bad idea. On the other hand, a diplomat will give you support by treating you with tact when your new hairstyle is unbecoming or when your bad decision is already made and it is too late to change. Like all of the traits I have been talking about, neither is necessarily better or worse. There are positive and negative sides to both.

BEFORE WE TRAVEL TO URANUS

This trait is related to the *need for affiliation* researched by David McClelland. How much do we care about what other people think of us? How important is it for us to have good relationships with other people? How much do other peoples' impressions of us matter to us?

This need has a tremendous impact on our cognitive and communication styles (how we think and how we speak). This last trait is probably affected by and affects all of the other traits I have discussed in chapters 1 through 8, because at the end of our analysis it all comes down to our conversation. What words do we use when we are trying to communicate with someone who is different from us? Paying attention to our basic communication style can take us a long way down the road to being more effective at work and in life.

Which End of the Spectrum Most Characterizes Me?

Do you tend to "tell it like it is"? Do you speak what you see as the unvarnished truth, and are you sometimes taken aback by charges of being harsh and abrasive when you see yourself as being helpfully straightforward? Or do you try to be diplomatic and tactful, only to find that sometimes people have totally misunderstood what you were trying to tell them?

Which End of the Spectrum Most Characterizes Those Closest to Me at Work: My Boss, My Co-Workers, My Peers, and My Employees?

Are there people you can go to when you really want to know the truth, even when it can hurt? Are these the same people you avoid at times for the same reason? What about the people you go to at work when you need a little sympathy and kindness? You may not get a lot of constructive criticism from them, but that may not be what you are looking for. If you are smart, you know where to go for what you need. I will explore that further in this chapter.

KAREN'S PALS ARE FROM URANUS

Karen has a serious problem. She has been in her new job for only two months, and it is becoming evident to her that she has made a mistake. She does not enjoy the work or the fast-paced environment, and she does not get along with her new boss. She is losing sleep and feeling ill over the stresses of her job.

Karen has two best friends, Marilyn and Kathie. When she confided in them, Kathie said, "I never liked the sound of that guy you work for, and you know he isn't going to change. Here's what you need to do. Let's get the Sunday paper this weekend and go through the want ads. We'll get on the computer too and send out your resume. I know you can find something else."

Marilyn said, "I'm so sorry it's not working out. I know that must be awfully stressful. So, do you want to go to the movies and out to lunch this weekend? It might help you get your mind off things for a while."

When Karen decided to stick it out for a while longer, Marilyn said, "I know you are the only one who can make this decision. Call me whenever you need to talk, and I'll be there for you." Kathie said, "I can't believe you're giving that job another chance. Does it have to kill you before you get the message?"

Kathie sees herself as the true friend that will tell you the truth, even when it hurts. She will tell you how to fix your problems and even fix them for you if you let her. Marilyn is the diplomat, a person who can be counted on to be tactful, empathize with you, and help by providing moral support.

Who is better for Karen? She needs both of them. If Karen is smart, she will realize what she needs and wants and draw on her two best friends for the support they can give. If Karen wants specific advice and the unvarnished truth (and a ride to the unemployment office), she needs to call Kathie. If she wants sympathy and support for her current course of action (whatever she decides that will be), she will call Marilyn.

Either person can be helpful or annoying, depending upon what Karen needs. If she is truly confused and wants advice, she needs to call Kathie. If she calls Marilyn, she is liable to still be confused. If she has made up her mind to give her job and her boss another chance, and she wants support and sympathy, she should call Marilyn. If she calls Kathie, she will be annoyed by the unsolicited advice. Understanding each person allows her to maintain these friendships without being frustrated or annoyed by them.

DISCREET URANUS: CHARACTERISTICS OF A DIPLOMAT

People can see a diplomat as a tactful, thoughtful, caring, sensitive person who is shrewd enough to realize the effect of his words on other people and can shape those words accordingly. Diplomats catch more flies with honey than with vinegar.

Being a diplomat is not all positive, however. Diplomats risk being seen as dishonest, unwilling to face facts, and underhanded. They may be accused of having a hidden agenda or being sneaky. Because they may not communicate directly or clearly, they run the risk of being misunderstood. Because they empathize with whatever course of action you decide to take, they sometimes hear, "But just tell me what I should do!"

HONEST URANUS: CHARACTERISTICS OF A TRUE FRIEND

A true friend is open and honest, straightforward, and forthright. True friends say what they mean and mean what they say. They are fond of expressions like "let's face the facts" and "let's lay the cards on the table."

A true friend risks being seen as pushy, heavy-handed, and rude. He may alienate other people and they may see him as annoying or difficult to be around. He may not see the need to deliver bad news or constructive criticism gradually, for example, so people walk away feeling wounded. He truly is trying to help and may feel hurt himself when his advice is spurned.

URANIAN COMBINATIONS

Let's look at the various combinations of two true friends, two diplomats, and one of each, and what these combinations can mean in the workplace.

Two True Friends

Two people who are straightforward, honest, and open tend to get along fine, right up until the time they butt heads. The good news is, neither one of them will take offense at being told to back off. They can remain good friends even when they are shouting at each other.

When one true friend says to another, "I can't believe you just said that! What a jerk!" the other one might reply, "What do you mean? What did I say?" The two can talk it out and resolve it on the spot. Because both have similar communication styles, neither will see the other as harsh or abrasive.

In the workplace, this communication style does not tend to affect the job at hand as much as it does the communication style with which the job gets done. And, as I said, the job gets done just fine with true friends at the helm. If there is disagreement as to how the job should be done, two true friends will hash out the problems quickly (perhaps loudly) and move on with no hard feelings.

Two Diplomats

Two diplomats can also get along fine. They are careful not to hurt each others' feelings and are careful about how they phrase things.

When one diplomat says to another, "You know, I was thinking about something you said the other day that kind of hurt my feelings," the other one gets the message loud and clear. Translated, this means, "I am very upset about something and have been stewing about it for days." A diplomat will respond by saying, "Oh no, what is it? You know I would never hurt your feelings on purpose."

The only issue in the workplace may occur when the job is unclear or if two diplomats disagree about how to proceed. They may spend additional time thrashing out such disagreements because they fear treading on each others' toes. In fact, they may proceed with the work without resolving major misunderstandings about what they are doing and why, which can lead to serious issues down the road. If two diplomats fail at an ambiguous task, a manager will often step in to give more direction and either not put these people on a task together in the future or be sure to give more explicit direction in the beginning.

One of Each

A true friend working with a diplomat is a relationship that can work out very well. It can also be a disaster. Suppose the two were having a conversation and one made a comment that hurt the other one's feelings. A diplomat might think about it for a while and then say, "You know, I was thinking about something you said the other day that kind of hurt my feelings." The true friend would not get the message that he hurt the diplomat's feelings, and no warning bells would go off. A true friend will treat this communication at face value—as an offhand statement of little importance.

If the tables were turned, a true friend would immediately say something like, "I can't believe you said that! What a jerk!" And most diplomats would be very hurt by this statement. They may withdraw from the conversation or from the person.

If the relationship survives long enough, the two may come

to understand each other's style and eventually can maintain a working or even social relationship. The best way for this relationship to thrive is for each side to shift her style a little bit. If there is something important to say, a diplomat needs to learn to get the true friend's attention in a stronger fashion. That may mean saying something like, "I really want to talk to you about something that happened yesterday." A true friend needs to tone it down also. The initial reaction ("You jerk!") needs to stay unsaid. Instead, he or she may count to ten and then say, "I really want to talk further about what you just said. It seems like you are saying that I was wrong to do what I did. Is that what you meant?"

In terms of getting the job done, the combination actually works very well because the true friend's own direct style can clear up any ambiguity in direction or task more efficiently than if she were not on the team.

Co-Workers. Co-workers are the siblings of the work world. So watch out! Sibling rivalry is a reality at work. With our bosses and our employees we have the formality of a reporting relationship, but with our co-workers we have the chaos of "equality." We are thrown into a sea of personality differences, we rarely get to choose our work partners, and personality conflicts tend to abound.

Communication style may be at the heart of some of these personality conflicts, and if they are, look closely for diplomats versus true friends. One of the ways we can identify the traits of people who resemble us is that we tend to like them. If you enjoy someone's company, work well with her, etc., chances are you share some of the same traits.

Essentially, everything in the "One of Each" section applies to co-workers, because their connection is not complicated by reporting relationships.

Boss and Employee. The next set of relationships is complicated, however. If the boss is a true friend and the employee is a diplomat, the relationship almost sounds traditional, doesn't it? The boss barks out orders with no concern for tact, and the subordinate politely complies. No problem, right?

Not so fast. As one might expect, there is a problem with the boss from Uranus. The true-friend subordinate may go away and do what he or she was ordered to do, but we have known for a long time that compliance with orders is a far cry from true commitment and motivation to work. An employee who feels browbeaten, mistreated, and misunderstood is not going to give 100 percent, treat customers well, care deeply about the mission of the company, and have deep loyalties to the boss.

If you are a manager and people do what you tell them to do, it may be very difficult to realize that there is a problem. You might think, "I say, 'Jump,' they say, 'How high?' No problem, right?" If you recognize yourself at all in the description of the true friend, please read the upcoming "How to Be More Balanced" sections carefully.

Employee and Boss. What if the boss is a diplomat and the employee is a true friend? This is a little less common but it can happen. And it can result in confusion and mixed signals. There are some bosses who are hard to read and whose messages take some time to interpret. If employees are accustomed to a boss from Uranus and they get a new boss who is a diplomat and tends to have a more tactful and diplomatic communication style, the employees may miss the boss's message altogether. The new boss might have to communicate in a more straightforward fashion simply because people misinterpret her natural style as weak or ineffective.

HOW TO BE MORE BALANCED IF YOU'RE A DIPLOMAT

Keep in mind that if you are a diplomat, you may be miscommunicating at work. If you are the boss, you are likely to make requests instead of demands and "soften" harsh feedback. That works well with fellow diplomats, but true friends won't get the message.

A manager I know was at his wit's end with some of his staff members. He told them what to do in what to him was plain language ("When you get a chance," and "Oh, by the way," and "You may want to consider."). One woman on his staff was a true friend, and she took his words at face value. When he asked her about a task, she would say, "I haven't had a chance yet," or, "Yes, I considered it and decided not to." To the manager, this was insubordination. To the employee, the situation was puzzling and frustrating. In fact, she ended up accusing the manager of being dishonest and sneaky by not telling her more straightforwardly what he wanted.

If you feel like those around you don't pay attention to you or don't understand you, you may simply be talking in language they can't translate. As a diplomat, you feel you are being tactful when you say things like, "You know, it kind of bothers me when you leave your newspapers all over our cubicle." Someone who is different from you on this personality trait and communication style literally doesn't hear you. What you meant to say is, "Please throw your newspapers into the trash in the mornings once you are done with them." That is not rude or harsh. You don't have to be rude to get your message across. Some people make the mistake of thinking that the opposite of diplomatic is, "I'm sick of you and your messy newspapers." You can be polite without being difficult to understand.

Have you ever had one of those co-workers who just doesn't take a hint? If you have co-workers like this, it is not his fault. It is yours. If he does not respond to subtle signals, he is probably a true friend. The important thing to remember about him is that he is fairly thick-skinned. He can take it if you say things that sound pretty blunt to you.

So as a co-worker who is a diplomat, think about those times that you have been misunderstood. It shouldn't be hard; it's those times you said something people ignored. Stop repeating yourself! It isn't working. You don't need to say it in a rude, harsh, or abrasive way; you just need to say it a little bit differently than you have been saying it. Consider these three steps along the Uranus spectrum, and choose the middle ground.

1. *"It sure would be nice to have the cubicle clean every morning."*

2. *"Could you throw your newspapers in the trash can before you leave in the evening, Keiko? Thanks."*

3. *"You're such a slob, Keiko; I'm sick and tired of your newspapers all over the cubicle floor every day."*

As a diplomat boss, you may think that you are the best kind of boss because you don't bark out orders like a dictator. But keep in mind, it can be frustrating to employees when they don't know exactly what you want from them. There is a middle ground here as well. When you are being too diplomatic, too tactful, or too indirect in your communication, employees don't know exactly what it is you want them to do or exactly what it is they did wrong, and they don't know how to fix it. There are times when direct communication is critical from a manager. It will ease your frustration and theirs. And again, you don't have to go all the way to Uranus to become a more direct communicator. Look at these three examples:

1. *"Susan, you may want to think about handling that kind of customer complaint a little differently."*

2. *"Susan, in the future, when a customer complains about a product like that, simply offer a refund or a replacement. It's best not to convince him that he's wrong about the product being bad. Thanks."*

3. *"Susan, are you out of your mind? Why in the world would you tell a customer that a product is just fine and try to convince her that she's wrong? Just give her a new one or her money back. Geez, how long have you worked here?"*

A diplomat employee with a true-friend boss faces special challenges as well. If you have problems, grievances, or issues that you want to discuss with your boss, you may feel unheard. It may simply be that you're not speaking the same language. You may state your issues in such terms that your boss doesn't take them seriously. If you say things like, "I was just thinking," or, "If you have a minute," or, "This isn't really a big deal, but," your boss is not going to take it seriously. If you have an issue to discuss with your boss, you need to state it somewhat more clearly and straightforwardly than you're used to doing. This is the way that you're going to get her attention. Again, let's look at a three-step example:

1. *"When you get a chance, boss, could we maybe talk about my schedule for next week? I've got this family thing coming up."*

2. *"Boss, my daughter's first birthday is next Saturday, and I would really appreciate it if I could get that day off."*

3. *"Boss, I can't work next Saturday."*

HOW TO BE MORE BALANCED IF YOU'RE A TRUE FRIEND

Do you have what seems to be an unearned reputation for being hard to get along with? Are you honestly puzzled by people's reactions to you at work? Look at your behavior in terms of the true-friend characteristics. If you consider yourself to be open, honest, and straightforward, yet some people find you annoying, decide first if it is something you want to change. Certainly, if you're annoying your boss or immediate co-workers, it might be to your benefit to get along better with them.

It's hard to change your basic personality. But try a couple of things. Try softening your message next time you give someone some feedback. Try saying "please" and "thank you." Try making changes to the words you use. Look at the following statement:

"It's ridiculous that we have to waste time on this project. Don't we all have enough to do? It obviously will never pay off anyway."

Now consider this:

"I have some major concerns about our current project. With our already full workloads, it isn't clear how we are going to free up the time to work on it. And as you can see by the forecasts I have attached, it seems as though the projected sales will not give us a return on our investment."

Same message, right? My reaction when reading the first one is to become defensive. When I see "It's ridiculous . . ." I think, "It is not!" and don't pay close attention to the rest of the memo. When I see the second one, I am much more apt to listen. Look how it starts off. The writer is taking responsibility for the opinion by starting with "I have some major concerns."

The first statement conveys strong opinion and emotion. The second conveys reasoned opinion and fact (note the phrase "the forecasts I have attached").

Let's look at some other examples. If you say to your co-worker something like, "I can't believe you just said that! What a jerk!" and your co-worker reacts with anger, tears, withdrawal, or some other defensive action, you are a true friend dealing with a diplomat. Instead of using the same tactics over and over again, try changing your tactics. It may feel funny to you at first, but try saying something like, "You know, I was thinking about something you said the other day that kind of hurt my feelings." If your co-worker reacts positively, you may have hit on something.

Think about it. Saying, "I'm sick of you and your messy newspapers," is rude, not honest. It is emotional and results in charged-up emotions in the other person. Tone it down a little. Practice ahead of time. Take the emotion out of it, and stick to the facts. Say something like, "When I got to work this morning, your newspapers were on the floor in our cubicle. I don't like putting them in the trash, and I don't like leaving them on the floor. Would you put them in the trash when you are done reading them?"

Have you had experiences with people becoming offended by you for reasons you just can't understand? You may be a true friend who needs to learn how to recognize diplomats. If uninvited guests drop by your office, you might have no problem saying, "Go away now, I have work to do." If they become offended, they are probably diplomats. Try subtle messages like glancing at the clock. Diplomats will get the message and gracefully excuse themselves.

True friends who want to moderate their style need to learn a repertoire of behaviors and escalate them as necessary. Don't start off by hitting someone over the head with a two-by-four. Learn a few more subtle techniques. Get to know your peers and associates, and know the ones who respond better to softer messages.

As a co-worker, you can assess which of your co-workers can deal with your style and which cannot. You can certainly tell by their reactions. Among those who don't deal well with your style, and among those with whom you need to deal better, work on changing your style just a bit. The three-step examples I talked about earlier work for diplomats as well as for true friends. Both need to try for the middle ground. You're not going to turn into a diplomat any more than a diplomat is going to turn into a true friend. But striving for the middle ground means no one is going to be rude and abrasive, and no one is going to be misunderstood, with any luck.

If you are a boss who is a true friend, it is going to be a bit difficult to change your style. People often think a boss's job is to bark out orders and be somewhat of a dictator. But we know that people are motivated to perform better, and have more of a true commitment to their jobs, if they are managed a bit differently. So it does pay off if you can back off from the dictatorship and change the perception (that some of your diplomat employees may have, anyway) that you tend to be a bit harsh and abrasive. How can you do that? Again, it is the middle ground that we are striving for. Try it a few times when you are not under a lot of stress and anxiety. The big deals, the big mistakes, the times of great stress for you—these are the times when your true colors are most likely to come out. Don't be too rough on yourself if these changes don't happen immediately. Practice during the quiet times. Practice whenever you can. That way when the tough times occur, you'll be more likely to take a deep breath, come down a bit from Uranus, and find that middle ground of communication style.

As a true friend employee with a diplomat boss, you will need to learn to translate. At first you may think that when your boss says things like, "When you have a chance," or "When you get around to it," or "You may want to think about," that he really means it. You will come to find out that these expressions don't mean what you think they mean. These kinds of expressions are just a polite way of giving you orders. And when he gives you the mildest of criticisms, you need to take that as serious feedback. Any other boss would be screaming at you. You may have co-workers who fill you in on this boss and his way of communicating, and you may not. You may have to learn over time.

Diplomats are actually difficult to work for, believe it or not. You may find yourself not being promoted, or you may find yourself receiving a bad performance review. You may find yourself not receiving other opportunities in the company and not knowing why. Up until this point, you might have thought you were doing fine and thought you worked for a great boss because life was so easy. You need to figure out a way to communicate with this boss, and again, sometimes the best way to do that is to be able to translate. Sometimes, not always, you can establish a rapport with this boss and get him to tell you exactly what you're doing well and what you're doing that requires improvement. Most of the time, however, you're going to have to learn his language and read between the lines, unless of course he reads this book and begins to communicate a bit more clearly. Perhaps you can loan him your copy!

 ## WHAT WE'VE LEARNED ON OUR TRIP TO URANUS

True Friend

Positive Characteristics. A true friend is open and honest, straightforward, and forthright. She will say what she means and mean what she says. You can count on her for constructive criticism.

Negative Characteristics. True friends can also be pushy, heavy-handed, rude, annoying, or difficult to be around. They can come across as harsh or abrasive at times.

What You Will Get from Them

- Specific advice
- Brutal honesty
- Constructive criticism

What You Need to Give Them

- Unvarnished truth
- Specific feedback
- Your open agenda

Diplomat

Positive Characteristics. Diplomats are tactful, thoughtful, caring, and sensitive. They communicate in ways that take the other person's feelings into account.

Negative Characteristics. People might see diplomats as dishonest, unwilling to face facts, underhanded, and sneaky. Sometimes people think they have hidden agendas.

What You Will Get from Them

- Empathy

- Moral support

- Possibly a hidden agenda

What You Need to Give Them

- Positive feedback

- Criticism within the framework of a relationship

- A positive atmosphere

AFTER OUR TRIP TO URANUS

This worksheet will help you think about the concepts presented in this chapter.

1. Which end of the spectrum most characterizes me?

True Friend ←————————————————→ **Diplomat**

2. How does this trait help me contribute positively to situations?

3. When do I need to "stretch" a bit in the opposite direction?

4. Which end of the spectrum most characterizes those closest to me at work? (If you have chosen to analyze your boss, particular co-workers, and/or employees who are particularly problematic for you at work, continue to analyze that person or persons here.)

MY BOSS

True Friend ← ────────────────── → **Diplomat**

MY CO-WORKERS

True Friend ← ────────────────── → **Diplomat**

MY PEERS

True Friend ← ────────────────── → **Diplomat**

MY EMPLOYEES

True Friend ← ────────────────── → **Diplomat**

5. How can I best call on these people when I need to use their natural abilities?

6. How can I avoid expecting them to do things that fly in the face of their natural style? How can I stop being disappointed in them or angry at them when they do what just comes naturally to them?

7. How can I change my behavior to get along better with these people?

CHAPTER 10
The Team Strength in Neptune

The planet Neptune is named after one of the more powerful gods in Roman mythology. He is often pictured with a three-pronged spear and is characterized as holding sway over the sea—an ocean god for an ocean-colored planet. (Neptune was known to the Greeks as Poseidon, who divided the world with his brothers, Zeus and Hades.) Neptune is notable for being the first planet discovered based on mathematical prediction rather than regular observations. This planet portrays the strength that can develop when the two personality types in this chapter work effectively together. One type thought there was a planet out there; the other type did all the calculations necessary to find it.

BIG THINKER/STICKLER FOR DETAIL

There are two different types of thinkers or people with two different cognitive styles. One type, which I will call the "big thinker," thinks in terms of *the big picture*, and *the overall con-*

cepts. The other type, which I will refer to as "sticklers for detail," *think in terms of the details.*

These two types need each other and, perhaps more than most types, irritate each other. One can think of a great plan and the other can take care of the details that may otherwise fall between the cracks. What each needs to do is develop an understanding of, and an appreciation for, the other's style. Together, these two types wield a tremendous amount of power to get things done. Alone, they tend to be somewhat ineffective. In this chapter, I will explore the implications of having both types in the workplace.

BEFORE WE TRAVEL TO NEPTUNE

This trait describes a difference in cognitive style. Big-picture thinkers start at the top. They see the forest, not the trees. They need to see the overall view before they get into the details, if they ever want to get into the details. They like to see how all the pieces fit together, and they like to see a top-down, overall, big-picture view of the situation before they're comfortable starting in on a task. In other words, they often like to start at the end and go backward. They may overlook the details altogether. They are never comfortable just jumping in on a task.

Sticklers for detail, on the other hand, like to start at the beginning and go step by step. They are what are known as linear thinkers, meaning that they like to go in a straight line. They want all of the details first. They are systematic and methodical in their approach, like a careful plan of action, and tend to build progressively with what is much more of the bottom-up approach as opposed to the top-down approach of the big thinkers. The sticklers for details, in fact, often overlook the broad concepts altogether, or are not interested in them.

Which End of the Spectrum Most Characterizes Me?

Do you like to start a task with the end in mind? Do you begin by asking, "What is our goal? Where do we want to be with this in a few years?" Or do you like knowing where to start? Do you feel a certain comfort in knowing how to get from A to B to

C? Are you the one in your work group who is always reminding others of how much time you have left, of appointments that others may have forgotten, are making sure that the room is locked up when you leave, etc.?

Which End of the Spectrum Most Characterizes Those Closest to Me at Work: My Boss, My Co-Workers, My Peers, and My Employees?

What about those around you at work? Are you beginning to recognize any of them in these descriptions so far? Do you have big-picture, conceptual thinkers who are always strategizing but letting the small details slip between the cracks? Or do you have people who are constantly worrying about the details but forgetting about the broader, strategic implications of their activities?

TWO SIDES OF NEPTUNE: "HERE WE GO AGAIN"

It's Monday morning again! You file into the meeting room with the rest of your work group, grab a bagel and some coffee, and take your favorite seat. The purpose of the meeting today, according to a memo sent around last week, is to plan your department's strategy for next year's marketing campaign.

Lakeesha, the manager, starts the meeting off. "I'd like to just open it up for some free-flowing brainstorming at first. What are some of your ideas for creative new things to do next year?"

Charles speaks first. "I've been giving it a lot of thought since you sent the memo about today's meeting. I'd like to see us do some entirely new things next year. And let's not be stale and old by going with what we think works. Why don't we go to the source? Let's start with a customer focus group, take the best ideas, and plan to implement the ideas in the first quarter."

Carmen replies, "That would mean a focus group would have to take place very soon, because it is already October. Have you checked the schedule for the use of the meeting rooms? They're pretty booked. Also, we'd need to videotape the focus groups. Have we gotten the equipment fixed yet? I know it wasn't in the budget for this year. And have you thought about who would implement the new ideas? If these 'new things' are too far off from what we are already doing, we may not have the staff knowledge or resources to even put them into place after we collect all of the information."

"Here we go again," you think. "Every meeting it's the same thing; these two butting heads and having the same old conversation." But this time, Lakeesha is ready for them.

"Before you go any further, let me stop you right there," she says. "We've all seen this before. Charles and Carmen both have good ideas and then end up getting annoyed at each other." The two were, in fact, showing visible signs of annoyance already. "Look at what is happening here. Charles has some excellent ideas. They are not detailed yet, but they point us in an interesting direction. Carmen makes some excellent points as well. Neither of you are going in the wrong direction; you simply are looking at the situation from different perspectives.

"Here is what we are going to do this year. Charles and Carmen, you are going to be the co-chairs of the planning committee. Together, you have everything it takes to make this work well. Charles, you are in charge of the ideas and Carmen, you are in charge of the details. You'll meet regularly, and by putting your heads together, I think we'll have the best marketing campaign that we've had in years. The rest of us will be available for whatever kind of help the two of you decide you'll need. But together, you two have what it will take to iron out your agendas and your plan. So the two of you get together and work it out."

Lakeesha is attempting to get these two different types of workers together, and if she succeeds, she will have put together a powerful team.

"NEPTUNE MUST BE THERE": CHARACTERISTICS OF BIG THINKERS

Big thinkers tend to be the visionaries and strategic thinkers; they see the "big picture" and the overarching concepts that form the big picture. They can see the forest but don't necessarily have an eye for the individual trees.

They tend to be imaginative and innovative. They don't

want to play by the rules, they want to bend or break the rules, or make up new ones. Big thinkers tend to learn in large jumps, take intuitive leaps almost randomly without necessarily making connections, and then suddenly "get it." Big thinkers may be able to solve problems quickly once they have grasped the concepts involved, but they may have difficulty explaining how they did it. This can cause problems if the big thinker is the manager of a work group that includes a number of sticklers for detail.

"MATHEMATICAL LOGIC WILL FIND NEPTUNE": CHARACTERISTICS OF THE STICKLER FOR DETAIL

The members of the detail patrol are the detail-oriented thinkers. They do see the trees. They have a need for structure, and they tend to take a very practical outlook on life. They are realistic, and they like to follow the rules that are in place. Sticklers for detail tend to gain understanding in linear steps, with each step following logically from the previous one. They tend to follow logical paths in finding solutions and like to start at the beginning.

NEPTUNIAN COMBINATIONS

How are two big thinkers going to get along in the workplace? What about two sticklers for detail? Let's explore those combinations, along with one of each.

Two Big Thinkers

Big thinkers enjoy one another's company. They have a great time discussing "what ifs." They tend to see each situation in terms of endless possibilities. They are missing the structure and detail of the sticklers for detail, and eventually that will come back to haunt them. After all, somebody has to take care of the details. Two (or more) big thinkers may find themselves caught short the day of the party, event, or business deal they had planned, because no one thought to take care of the myriad of little details that causes the plan to go smoothly.

In other words, the conflict between two big thinkers working together is not a result of a personality clash; it's because together they are missing some key ingredients in getting the task completed in a way that ties together all of the loose ends. They work together in harmony but not necessarily effectively.

Two Sticklers for Detail

Sticklers for detail get along well with one another. They are very comfortable drilling down to the level of detail that both are satisfied with. The downside is that they are missing the big-picture perspective. And the biggest problem is that they don't know it is missing. They may do well planning the day-to-day detail, if that's what is necessary, but when it comes time for strategic thinking and planning for the company, they may be caught short.

So here, too, the conflict is not between them but with the broader organization. They may complete the task itself impeccably, but it may not be in line with the organizational objectives. It may not support the organization's long-term strategic goals. Like the big thinkers, they get along just fine but may not do the best job together.

One of Each

Big thinkers and sticklers for detail need each other! The dichotomy simply cries out for a team because the power of getting these two types together is so great. One can think of a great plan, the other can take care of the details that may otherwise fall between the cracks. What each needs to do is develop an understanding of, and an appreciation for, the other's style. The difficulty here is that one finds the other annoying. When they work together, you may hear the big-picture people accuse the sticklers of nit-picking, and the sticklers might accuse the big-picture people of having their heads in the clouds.

This is exactly why they need each other, of course. Big thinkers who can't see the details may have serious problems. Even after they have the strategic plan in place, they may be fuzzy on the details, so the best of plans may fall by the wayside and not come to fruition. And even when the sticklers for detail have all the details in place, they have trouble relating them to the big picture, so that the organization might not adopt the plan because it does not support the organizational strategy.

How do we come to this level of understanding, appreciation, and even trust? It is simple, but not easy. Everyone must realize that each type is not trying to resist the other, annoy the other, or block action from taking place. Sometimes it takes a few failures to realize that we cannot simply work on a team full of people whom we get along well with, because if we do, we are missing things that only people with different cognitive styles can see. I advise people to be careful about new teams on which they feel an instant camaraderie ("We all just get along so well!"). If you all think alike, you may have problems. You may want to invite someone onto the team whom you find a bit annoying. Why? Because that person sees things differently than you do, and you need that person. He is the one who will keep you in line, so to speak, and you will eventually come to appreciate it at the eleventh hour when the pieces your team would otherwise have missed turn out to be in place after all.

Co-Workers. So how can Charles and Carmen (from our opening case study) work together most effectively on the new marketing campaign? Clearly, their manager has seen that when they put their heads together they add up to the best of both worlds. That is, as long as they can keep from annoying each other and hurling accusations of nit-picking or head-in-the-clouds impracticality.

In our case study, their manager has given them some good instructions to start. With a little respect and understanding of each other's strengths, big-thinker Charles can lay out the goal, the objectives, and the intent of the campaign; detail-oriented Carmen can fill in the blanks. In fact, if they understand and respect each other's weaknesses, Carmen can quit expecting Charles to pay attention to the details, and Charles can quit being annoyed at Carmen for failing to see and appreciate the big picture concepts that are so dear to his heart. Charles can make sure the details align with the objectives and strategies of the organization, and Carmen can make sure Charles's ideas can be carried out given the constraints of time, cost, budget, and other scheduling details.

Boss and Employee. What if the boss is a big thinker and has a staff full of sticklers for detail? As I said earlier, big thinkers tend to take intuitive leaps of logic and solve problems without even being able to explain how they got there. This can make it difficult for a leader to convince the sticklers for detail to follow him down a path. Sometimes the big thinker finds himself leading the parade with no followers. The sticklers for detail are still at the beginning of the path, trying to fit A to B to C in a linear fashion. I will talk more about how to deal with this in the "How to Be More Balanced" section. Essentially, a leader is not a leader if she has no followers. Sometimes she needs to create a path toward her solution even when she made a leap and failed to forge a path. Few sticklers for detail will simply close their eyes and take that leap with her on trust alone.

Employee and Boss. What if you are a boss who is a stickler for detail and you find yourself with a staff full of big thinkers? Of course, you have the power of the position and can probably have things your way. But there are two things to think about. First of all, your linear thinking and your insistence on starting at the beginning is serving your needs, not your staff's needs. You are frustrating your staff unnecessarily. Second, these big thinkers have a great deal to offer you. As a manager, you do need to think strategically more often than you probably do. You may want to do your detail work prior to your conversations with your staff, tune in to their big-picture thinking, and use it to your advantage.

HOW TO BE MORE BALANCED

This may be one of the more difficult traits in which to become more balanced. This is a cognitive style that seems to be very inherent to the way that we work. And it has little to do with our intelligence or our emotional intelligence, although it has some ties to our personality, and it is very much simply a part of our unconscious way of thinking.

Let me give you an example. I was going to do some work for a well-known leadership training and development organization. When I showed up for its one-week training session, I was directed to park in the underground parking garage, a five-level structure. There were signs throughout the garage, which I discovered later indicated a speed limit of four miles per hour throughout the garage. Being a big-picture thinker and not detail-oriented, I parked, saw a sign with a four on it and assumed I was on level four of the garage. Needless to say, that made finding my car at the end of the day a bit of a challenge. I did discover after the first day that the signs indicating the level were different from the signs indicating the speed limit. But I did have to make a special effort each day to remember which level and which side of the garage I'd parked on. So I would stand at the elevator each morning saying to myself, "Level two on the right, level two on the right," so that at the end of the eight-hour day I would remember where I had parked.

A couple of years later, some colleagues and I were talking about a test that we gave to the leaders who attended this leadership-seminar training. It was a test called "Hidden Figures," where geometric shapes appeared on a piece of paper and a larger complex figure was either embedded within the shape or was not. The participant needed to indicate whether he or she could find the hidden figure within the larger shape. This was a test to determine whether the person was a big thinker or a stickler for detail. People who are very detail-oriented can pick out the hidden figures very easily, and the big-picture, conceptual thinkers cannot.

One man I worked with was such a big thinker that he failed the test altogether. He was the only one I had ever worked with who received a zero on the test. I was speculating with a colleague that I would probably receive a fairly low score myself and related to her the parking-garage story. She said that it was easy for her to remember where she parked. She just looked at the space number. "For example, today I'm in number 137," she told me. I said, with some amazement (and remember I'd been working there for two years), "The spaces are numbered?" The colleague I was talking to was clearly extremely detail-oriented, as she had noticed from the outset that the spaces were numbered in the parking garage. I was clearly a big thinker, having not even been able to recognize what level I was parked in.

If You're a Big Thinker

As a co-worker, if you are a big thinker, the most basic thing for you to do is accept the fact that you need the big picture of a task before you can even think about the details. If your co-workers start plunging directly into details, it can cause problems for you. If you are surrounded by sticklers for detail, you may want to get the meeting agenda or a task description ahead of time, so that you can do some of the prework and strategic thinking on your own. This takes a bit more time, but it will prepare you for the meeting because you will have done the top-down work that is so critical for you. It enables you to sit patiently in a meeting while linear thinkers take over.

As I said earlier, you can lead the parade, but that doesn't do much good if no one is following you. When you are the boss and you're getting ready to present a new strategy or a new idea to your employees, you may even want to invite one of the sticklers for detail in to help you plan the meeting. Ask questions like, "What would help this make sense to you?" or "What more information would you need here?" Because you don't naturally think this way, identify the people around you who do and tap into them for assistance. And begin to learn from them while you do this. It doesn't hurt to be a little more well-rounded so that when you have meetings in the future you can connect with everyone in the audience, not just the big thinkers like yourself.

As a big-thinker employee who may have a stickler for detail as a boss, it is probably frustrating at times. Just remember, she's the boss. You may at times have to go back and create a linear path for her to follow; that is, if you want to sell your ideas. If you're in this position, I'm sure you have experienced the frustration of bouncing into her office with a wonderful new idea, only to be met with a blank stare. That's because your boss is not following the same leaps of logic that are so exciting to you. She wants to start at the beginning. She wants to see the steps and start from the bottom up.

If you simply can't do it, enlist the help of a stickler for detail from your work group and see if you can figure out the best way to approach your boss. In other words, find someone that speaks her language. While you're getting that help, learn. I know it's a foreign language, but you can pick up some tips that will help you the next time you need to approach your boss with a new idea. This will also help you when and if you are promoted to a supervisory or management position and have to speak this language to your own employees.

If You're a Stickler for Detail

As a co-worker, you may find yourself working with big thinkers who jump around from thought to thought and start talking strategically in a top-down manner. That leaves you quite confused. If you have lots of co-workers like that, you may have to do some homework outside of the meeting. As suggested for the big thinker, get the agenda or a description of the project ahead of time and fill in some of the details yourself. Do your linear thinking, and fill in the steps from A to B to C prior to attending a strategic-planning meeting. Outline the meeting information for yourself in logical order. In the long run, doing so will save you time and frustration, and it may improve your relationships with your colleagues. You might even strengthen your big-picture thinking skills. The more you can do so, the more well-rounded a team member you are likely to be.

As a stickler-for-detail boss, you have a lot of opportunities here. A manager really needs to be more tuned in to the strategic direction of an organization. The big thinkers on your staff, and I assume among your peers, have a lot to teach you. Your detail work is valuable to the organization, and it needs to be done. But it needs to be done prior to meetings and conversations with your staff. They need the bare-bones outline and will be frustrated by receiving a great deal of detail. Remember, although you may need it, they don't. What you want to do in meetings is tune in to the big-picture thinking and use it to your advantage. Ask questions that sound foreign to you and may even make you a little nervous. Ask questions like, "Where do you see us in five years?" or "What is the ultimate outcome we expect of this?"

As an employee who may be a stickler for details and finds herself working for a big-thinker manager, your best bet is to prove your value while not making yourself annoying. And you can be of great value. Your boss needs someone to take care of the details that he doesn't want to take care of. Volunteer to do things like schedule meetings, keep track of audits, and anything that you know a big-picture person is going to dislike and that would come easily to you. Don't bring things up in meetings that you know are going to cause eyes to roll and heavy sighs to be pointed in your direction. Learn to read the signs of annoyance in your boss. Let your strengths become of value to him. At the same time, begin to learn from him and the other big thinkers around you. If you aspire to a supervisory or management position, keep in mind that most people in those positions need to practice some kind of strategic or big-picture thinking in order to run organizations. So, in turn, tune in to the big-picture thinking that's going on around you and learn from that.

 WHAT WE'VE LEARNED ON OUR TRIP TO NEPTUNE

Big Thinker

Positive Characteristics. Big thinkers are able to, as the saying goes, think outside the box. They can redefine problems, come up with many good ideas, and break through what organizations or their colleagues see as restraints. They can be quite innovative and come up with new ways of thinking.

Negative Characteristics. Big thinkers can also experience problems because it's difficult to get those who are different from them to see outside the box. They can be met with a lot of resistance, and possibly skepticism, which irritates them to the point where they may start to act in a condescending manner. They might say things like, "I can see all of this so clearly; what is wrong with you people?"

Others in the organization may see them as undisciplined and impractical. This can escalate to the point where they can actually be, or seem, abrasive or insensitive in their efforts to be innovative.

What You Will Get from Them

- Innovation
- Strategic thinking
- Big ideas

What You Need to Give Them

- The whole picture
- The general idea, then the specifics
- Freedom from what they see as petty restrictions

Stickler for Detail

Positive Characteristics. The sticklers for detail can be very resourceful and often come up with great solutions to ongoing usual problems. They will tend to work within the rules and don't like sudden changes or new and exciting solutions. They are dependable and reliable and work in an orderly and organized fashion.

Negative Characteristics. The flip side of these positive traits means that people can see sticklers for detail as unimaginative, resistant to change, and lacking the big-picture views that the big thinker sees as so critical. People may see them as focused on the problem rather than on the solution.

What You Will Get from Them

- Steady, dependable work
- Attention to detail
- Logical and linear thinking

What You Need to Give Them

- The details
- Small incremental steps
- The specifics, then the general idea

AFTER OUR TRIP TO NEPTUNE

This worksheet will help you think about the concepts presented in this chapter.

1. Which end of the spectrum most characterizes me?

Big Thinker ➤ **Stickler for Detail**

2. How does this trait help me contribute positively to situations?

3. When do I need to "stretch" a bit in the opposite direction?

4. Which end of the spectrum most characterizes those closest to me at work? (If you have chosen to analyze your boss, particular co-workers, and/or employees who are particularly problematic for you at work, continue to analyze that person or persons here.)

MY BOSS

Big Thinker ➤ **Stickler for Detail**

MY CO-WORKERS

Big Thinker ➤ **Stickler for Detail**

MY PEERS

Big Thinker ➤ **Stickler for Detail**

Big Thinker   **Stickler for Detail**

5. How can I best call on these people when I need to use their natural abilities?

6. How can I avoid expecting them to do things that fly in the face of their natural style? How can I stop being disappointed in them or angry at them when they do what just comes naturally to them?

7. How can I change my behavior to get along better with these people?

THE TEAM STRENGTH IN NEPTUNE

CHAPTER 11
Plutonian People

Smaller than our own moon, Pluto has an interesting history. Long before people discovered or even observed it, they saw its effects and hypothesized its presence. It is similar to a person who works behind the scenes and does not seek glory for his own sake. Pluto was named after the ancient Roman god of the underworld, which also supports the "hidden" theme. First observed in 1930, Pluto became the subject of vigorous debate in 2006 and was demoted to the status of "dwarf planet."

Interestingly enough, the main reason for Pluto's demotion in 2006 was the fact that it did not have enough influence on its surroundings. The other eight planets are large enough and influential enough to pull other objects into their gravitational orbits, and Pluto is not. In fact, Neptune's gravitational pull influences Pluto's orbit more than was previously discovered. This makes it fit even more distinctly into the category of the "behind the scenes" person at work who is content to follow in someone else's shadow.

SELF-ASSURED/SELF-CRITICAL

There are some people in the workplace who have a high need for achievement and who tend to seek recognition and glory. There are others who work quietly behind the scenes, who do not feel the need to seek promotions or achievements, yet who are sometimes the backbone of their organizations. Let's explore these two types of people. For the sake of this chapter I will call them the *self-assured*, for those who work behind the scenes, and the *self-critical*, for those who are so ambitious that nothing is quite ever good enough.

People who have a *need for achievement* tend to be not only *ambitious*, but *self-critical*. Their motto may well be "I perform, therefore I am." They have a high level of aspiration and a need for advancement that accompanies their need for achievement. They tend to judge themselves based on their achievements— and not yesterday's, by the way! They tend to ask themselves, "What have I achieved today?"

The *self-assured* person, on the other hand, is *self-satisfied* and not as susceptible to guilt and anxiety if he does not accomplish his goals. His motto may be *"I am, and that's good."* He has a *healthy ego*, in other words. He does not base his self-esteem on his accomplishments and does not have a high need for achievement.

Once again, what we need to do here is understand the other person's point of view and foster a perspective that "my way" is not the only way or necessarily even the normal way.

BEFORE WE TRAVEL TO PLUTO

To understand this trait, I look to David McClelland's research and theory of motivation. He tells us that there are three motivators of human behavior (see introduction): achievement, power, and affiliation. In this chapter, I am going to look at the differences in behavior that result when individuals have a high need for achievement versus a low need for achievement.

The key to understanding this chapter, and to understanding people with a lower need for achievement, is that they are not "slackers" or people who lack ambition. We may be talking about people who are very good workers. And who, as I mentioned, may be the backbone of their organizations. They may be dependable, conscientious, and productive. We are simply talking about people who do not define their lives or their worth by their accomplishments at work. They may not show a lot of competitiveness or always look for that next promotion.

Which End of the Spectrum Most Characterizes Me?

Do you feel some degree of anxiety about getting things done at work? Do you feel personally involved, to the extent that you feel guilty if the work doesn't get done? Do you feel a great deal of personal satisfaction when work gets done well? Do you enjoy receiving feedback when the job was well done? Or do you just simply shrug it off at the end of the day and go home? Do you see work tasks more as "just your job"?

Which End of the Spectrum Most Characterizes Those Closest to Me at Work: My Boss, My Co-Workers, My Peers, and My Employees?

Do you feel that those around you at work tend to take their jobs very seriously, or do they see their work as "just a job"? Do they tend to throw themselves into their work and personally identify with the job and their achievements? Or do they seem more involved with outside activities and have more of the "nine-to-five" mentality?

Let's talk about how we can deal with both ends of the spectrum at work.

PLUTO'S PUZZLE: TO BE PITIED OR TO BE VALUED?

Kwan Kim has recently been hired to be the manager of the training department for a gas-and-electric company in a medium-size city. He is excited about the opportunity to make a difference in the department. One of his projects in the first few weeks on the job was meeting with each of the six employees in the department and talking with them about their jobs, where they saw themselves fitting in with the department, and what their aspirations were.

He had been particularly looking forward to meeting with Jessie, a 15-year employee who has been doing the same job since the day she was hired. Jessie is in charge of training the newly hired employees for the customer service phone bank. It is fairly intensive five-week training. The new employees are trained to answer calls from customers regarding hooking up their service, canceling their service, service outages, questions on their bills, etc. Kwan felt sorry for Jessie, thinking how limited he would feel if he was doing the same job for 15 years. Actually, he probably would have been so frustrated by now that he would have quit the company and looked for something else long ago. He was very excited about the idea of giving her some new opportunities and some new tasks. So on the day of their meeting, he jumped into the conversation fairly quickly.

"Let's talk about how we can further develop you," said Kwan. "First of all, I'd love to see you get more involved in things like training new supervisors or running some of the ongoing management training seminars. We could also use you over in some of the training we do for the newly hired technical employees. Are there any seminars you'd like to attend, some training you'd like to get in other areas, or . . . ," he stopped talking, taken aback by the look of thinly disguised horror on the employee's face.

"I'm not quite sure how to say this," said Jessie, after a pause. "Allison, the manager who was here before you, understood this. I really like the new-hire training. I feel like I'm pretty good at it, and the new hires like me and trust me. You can look at the surveys they fill out at the end of the training class. You can look at my annual appraisals from Allison."

"Oh no," said Kwan. "I wasn't saying in any way that you weren't good at what you do. I was just hoping that we might develop your skills in other areas."

"Well, that's just it," said Jessie. "I'm doing fine here. I like my job a lot. I don't really want to do anything else. It would just add a lot of stress to my life that I don't need. I have two teenage girls at home, and I'm very involved in their activities. Really, I'm fine."

Kwan started to get the message. Jessie wasn't saying it, but the message was, "Leave me alone." Just because Kwan would have felt very limited by doing the same job for 15 years—frustrated enough to look around for something else, even frustrated enough to leave the organization—that didn't mean that Jessie felt that way. In fact, just the opposite was true. Jessie was very happy doing her job and in fact was very good at it. Kwan was lucky to have her.

CONTENTED PLUTONIANS: CHARACTERISTICS OF THE SELF-ASSURED PERSON

It is tempting for high achievers to look at the self-assured person as someone who is not motivated. Instead, let's look at this person as someone who has a healthy ego and is self-satisfied. This person is not necessarily motivated by her work achievements. Like Jessie, perhaps she has other things going on in her life that meet her needs. She doesn't need constant high achievement in her work tasks to feel good about herself. She doesn't need to be promoted or pursue status at work in order to feel fulfilled.

Remember, McClelland talked about other needs as well. Perhaps Jessie has a high need for power and feels that her job allows her to wield power over the new hires that she deals with every five weeks. Or perhaps Jessie has a high need for affiliation, and the fact that the new hires depend on her so fully for what they need to succeed in the organization, and are so grateful to her when the training is over, meets that need. Jessie regularly receives thank-you notes, flowers, and other small gifts from the graduates of her training program. They stop in to her office years later to talk about how much the training meant to them, and she maintains relationships with employees who participate in the training program. That is very important to her. As we've seen, people who need power or affiliation act quite differently in the workplace than people who need achievement.

AMBITIOUS PLUTONIANS: CHARACTERISTICS OF THE SELF-CRITICAL PERSON

Self-critical people, on the other hand, depend on achievement to feel good about themselves. These people need challenging work situations and respond well to them. They seek situations where they can attain a sense of accomplishment and possibly advance.

Self-critical people tend to avoid both very high-risk and very low-risk situations. When the risks are very high the chances of failure are also high, and remember, this person has a high need for achievement, so he doesn't want to risk failure. Conversely, when the risk is very low, there is not a lot of value in the achievement. Easy tasks do not motivate these people or make them feel that they have achieved anything and therefore are not of value for them. High achievers also like regular feedback so they know how they're doing. They like to receive kudos for a job well done—external validation that they did well on a task.

Kwan's perception was that anything a person had done for 15 years would come too easily and therefore would not be challenging. He assumed that this person would need a new challenge, because he would. He would also not throw Jessie into a task that she was not ready for, but he would offer her training and development. In other words, he would not set her up for failure, he would help her achieve.

PLUTONIAN COMBINATIONS

Let's look at what happens when two self-assured people work together, and two self-critical people, and then one of each.

Two Self-Assured People

Two self-assured people will have very little problem getting along in the workplace. Jessie and a co-worker just like her would be very effective in running the new-hire training sessions. The problem would not be between the co-workers but between that department or team and the larger organization.

For instance, self-assured people might work dependably, doing their jobs and doing them well. The organization, however, might have very little idea of what they do and how they do it. These self-assured people see no reason to seek any glory for their accomplishments or to "shine the light" on their achievements. Unless they have a manager who seeks such glory for them, they are liable to suffer during budget cuts, or even headcount cuts, because executives and other decision makers in the organization may have very little idea of the value that they actually bring to the organization. The self-assured people (who, as I mentioned, may be the backbone of the organization) tend not to be the shining stars of the organization simply because they don't seek recognition and status. They may tend to be invisible to the higher levels.

Two Self-Critical People

So now let's look at the situation where we have two self-critical people (that is, two people with a high need for achievement) working together. These are people who will set challenging goals, be competitive, and ultimately do very good work— hypothetically. They can also, depending on their degree of competitiveness, sabotage each other. Remember, these are people who want to win. Depending upon their degree of self-promotion, they may promote themselves at the expense of their co-workers. There is the potential for some conflict here. The variables in the organization partly determine the degree of conflict. For instance, the self-critical person might wonder what kinds of opportunities there are there for advancement. Does the reward system in the organization promote collaboration or competition? If the opportunities are few and far between, and the competitiveness is fierce, the self-critical people will tend to be far less cooperative with one another than they might be otherwise. In organizations with lots of opportunities for advancement, these people may be far more likely to work together cooperatively because both of them (or all of them) see plenty of opportunities.

Self-critical people may also be a bit unrealistic in setting their goals. They are so motivated by new and exciting challenges that they may be bored by doing the "same old thing." The problem is, someone has to do those things! If there happens to be a team of self-critical co-workers who are responsible for some mundane, repetitive tasks, we run the risk of seeing them neglect these tasks when something new and exciting comes along. And when self-critical people work on a team, sometimes the risk is less to themselves than it is to the broader organization. Unless someone, their bosses perhaps, are keeping a close eye on things, the risk is that the repetitive, mundane, yet critical tasks may fall between the cracks while the new and exciting tasks receive all of the attention.

One of Each

In situations where we have self-assured and self-critical people working together, there are any number of ways such scenarios can play out. Let's look at some examples.

Co-Workers. In a peer relationship, the self-assured individual is often content to work in the shadow of the self-critical or high-achieving individual. It may not look equitable or fair to the outside observer, but it also doesn't last long because the high achiever frequently moves on, through promotions or lateral movements to other departments.

For example, in our opening case study, there are five other people who work in the training department with Jessie. None of them have been there as long as she has. One job in particular, the management-development specialist, has been a bit of a re-volving door. The people who take that position tend to move on in two to three years. Why? We can assume that these people are more self-critical types. They tend to come in, take on a lot of responsibilities, play the political game very well, and either get promoted or leave the organization for another position else-where. They get along very well with Jessie. She orients them to the department, helps them with any questions they have, and is a great source of information on departmental history, customs, where to find supplies, how to order equipment, etc. They too, often keep in touch with Jessie after they leave.

Where is the potential for conflict here? It does exist. Some of the high achievers who move through the training depart-ment find themselves becoming somewhat annoyed with Jesse. Like Kwan, they feel the urge to push Jessie a bit. They feel somewhat uneasy that she has been there that long, and they urge her to do something different, something more. Although they may like her, they can't help but view her a bit negatively as they look at the years she has spent in the department and compare her accomplishments in the organization with their own. They get annoyed when she resists their suggestions to ask for promotions, attend developmental seminars, etc. And if they work with her long enough, their annoyance does set up a bit of a barrier between them.

And Jessie, of course, is in turn eventually annoyed by those self-critical people. Why can't they just do their jobs well and quit worrying about the next promotion to come along? Jesse's first concern is her department. So she may come to view the self-critical people negatively when they continue to turn their attention outward and take what she sees as an excessive interest in the outside world rather than paying enough attention to their current roles.

Boss and Employee. If the boss is self-assured, she is often willing to promote and develop the self-critical employee. This is a great kind of a boss to have, by the way, if you are a person with a high need for achievement. This kind of boss will let you find opportunities, allow you to develop, and let your name stay in the spotlight.

You may wonder how a self-assured person becomes a manager. It does happen. Often, if a person is very good at getting the job done, she becomes valuable to the organization and is promoted on the basis of her ability. Jessie, for example, might eventually get promoted to manage the department whether she actually steps forward to apply for the position or not. Depending upon what was going on in her life at the time, she may accept the position and may even do a very good job at it. And, as noted, her self-critical employees can stay in the spotlight and she will even help them do so.

And what is the potential for conflict? If Jessie is the supervisor of the department at some point, she will not really see the need for all of the opportunities, achievements, and advancements that her self-critical employees are looking for. They are liable to confuse, exhaust, and annoy her with their constant pushing. And she, of course, is undoubtedly going to annoy them by not taking their requests seriously enough.

Employee and Boss. The self-critical boss, who is looking to promote himself and is looking for his own advancement opportunities, is usually not a problem for the self-assured employee. The self-assured employee, like Jessie, may have a long career and have several self-critical bosses because they tend to move through the organization quickly, either through promotion or through quitting in frustration due to lack of promotions.

The self-critical boss, in fact, often fits the typical managerial profile. This person is a high achiever driven by a desire for advancement. The problem that may arise is if the person's desire for advancement comes at the cost of the attention he pays to his own department. Perhaps he is too busy playing the organizational politics or trying to get promoted to pay enough attention to his employees' well-being or to the ongoing needs of his own department.

And this situation may plant the seeds of conflict. The employee who is self-assured and is working away dependably at his job is oftentimes frustrated by the boss, who is ambitiously working toward his next promotion and ignoring the real needs of his own department in the meantime. The employee can become resentful and remind the boss of what the department needs, and the boss can become annoyed at these petty details and wonder why the employee can't just take care of them himself.

HOW TO BE MORE BALANCED

It is sometimes difficult to think about balance in all of the personality traits, motivational styles, and characteristics that I've been talking about. All of them are so inborn and inherently part of us. This trait is no different. But if we can be more effective by adjusting our behavior just a little bit, why not think about it? Here are some tips to ponder.

If You're Self-Assured

As a co-worker, you may do a good job and do it well, but you also may be doing your department a disservice by staying in the shadows. Sometimes seeking a little glory is the politically correct thing to do. In an organization that pays attention to achievement, you may need to seek a few more challenges and draw more attention to your achievements if you want to get the right budget and headcount for your department. For instance, Jessie may receive lots of little thank-you notes and other gifts from her grateful students, but unless the executive decision makers in the organization know about her value to the organization, she runs the risk of having her budget cut, or even her training program eliminated, because only her students know about her value. In addition, her co-workers might see her as a more valuable team player if she occasionally expresses some enthusiasm for the things that interest them: seminars, workshops, and other developmental activities.

If you're a boss, the previous paragraph applies to you even more. Being effective within your department is certainly part of your job, but managing the image of your department in the broader organization is a large part of your job as well. Remember how the planet Pluto was demoted because it didn't have enough influence on its surroundings? You need to exert some gravitational force on your surroundings. You do that by acting a bit more like the high achievers act, even if that does not come naturally to you. You need to get out there and run a political campaign on behalf of your department. You need to somehow not only achieve, but figure out a way to advertise those achievements. A good boss is concerned about his employees and the day-to-day running of his department. A great boss also focuses his attention on the broader organization and makes sure that the broader organization knows what his department is capable of. And do pay some attention to those self-critical employees of yours; they are not pushing for achievement or advancement just to annoy you, those things are an important part of their motivational makeup. You can utilize them to bring glory to your department; just don't plan on having them for long.

As an employee, keep in mind that sometimes your self-assured behavior may come across to your boss as unmotivated. Particularly to a new boss, you may want to express enthusiasm and interest a bit differently than you usually do. You may want to say yes to some new tasks, or even a new promotion, not because you really wanted it but because it may help the department. Figure out a subtle way to promote yourself from time to time. When you receive those thank-you notes from your customers or other employees, post them in your cubicle. Let your boss know of your accomplishments. Let your boss's boss know of your accomplishments. Next time the opportunity arises, go ahead and volunteer to be on that task force or committee that you've always said no to.

If You're Self-Critical

If you are someone with a high need for achievement, this is something that is just an inherent part of you, and it is not going to change. But let's think about some ways that you might adjust your behavior at times to make you more effective. As a co-worker, sometimes you may seem a bit overbearing to those around you and the others on your team, especially if you work with people who are less self-critical than you are. You may sometimes want to tone it down a bit in your talk about setting goals and trying to do things just a little bit more or a little bit better. You may sometimes want to think about the task at hand and simply work on it with your co-workers, even if it is a bit boring and repetitive. They may not want to hear about how much you're looking forward to that next promotion, or how boring it is to be doing the same work that you did last year.

As a boss, yes, your job is to be the high achiever, set high goals, and hold high standards for yourself, your employees, and your department. Just be careful that it doesn't get in the way of your effectiveness today, right now, in your department. Are you always thinking about the next job, the next big thing, the next promotion? Take a look right now, today, at your employees and your department. When was the last time you sat down with your employees and asked them what they needed from you? When was the last time you focused your attention inward? That is every bit as important as the focus on your next move.

As an employee, you may want to think more about what your boss wants of you. There isn't anything wrong with having high aspirations and setting high goals. But speak frankly with your boss about what is required of you right now. You can also, of course, speak frankly about where you want to go from here and what you think your next promotion ought to be. But sometimes the best way to get that promotion is to be very effective at your current job, and sometimes that means doing the boring, repetitive tasks for a while.

 ## WHAT WE'VE LEARNED ON OUR TRIP TO PLUTO

Self-Assured

Positive Characteristics. The self-assured person has a healthy ego and does not define himself or his worth by his accomplishments. He tends to take a relaxed approach to life and work.

Negative Characteristics. People may not see the self-assured person as the most motivated person on the job. He may not create a lot of positive public relations for his department, because no one is really aware of what he has accomplished.

What You Will Get from Them

- Self-satisfaction

- A healthy ego

- Noncompetitiveness

What You Need to Give Them

- Appreciation

- Lack of pressure

- Ability to move at their own pace

Self-Critical

Positive Characteristics. The self-critical person is achievement-oriented, goal-oriented, and tends to take his job very seriously.

Negative Characteristics. Because the self-critical person is a high achiever, he expects that others are the same. Like most of us, he thinks his own feelings are normal. In an organization, however, this can be disruptive because he holds high standards and holds himself to high expectations. He expects others around him to feel the same way. This of course can be annoying to the people around him who don't hold the same high standards. He may have to develop patience and the people skills necessary to work with those around him who have a lower need for achievement than he has.

What You Will Get from Them

- Strong desire for achievement
- Ability to set high personal goals
- Desire for advancement

What You Need to Give Them

- Feedback
- Opportunities for advancement
- Opportunities for achievement

AFTER OUR TRIP TO PLUTO

This worksheet will help you think about the concepts presented in this chapter.

1. Which end of the spectrum most characterizes me?

Self-Assured ⟷ **Self-Critical**

2. How does this trait help me contribute positively to situations?

3. When do I need to "stretch" a bit in the opposite direction?

4. Which end of the spectrum most characterizes those closest to me at work? (If you have chosen to analyze your boss, particular co-workers, and/or employees who are particularly problematic for you at work, continue to analyze that person or persons here.)

MY BOSS

MY CO-WORKERS

MY PEERS

MY EMPLOYEES

5. How can I best call on these people when I need to use their natural abilities?

6. How can I avoid expecting them to do things that fly in the face of their natural style? How can I stop being disappointed in them or angry at them when they do what just comes naturally to them?

7. How can I change my behavior to get along better with these people?

CHAPTER 12
Back to Earth

We have explored eleven personality traits, cognitive styles, and communication styles. Although I have discussed each of the characteristics separately, each person is, of course, a combination of all of them. For each situation in which you would like to improve your relationship with someone else, it is important that you take some time to figure out which of these characteristics is getting in the way or causing the problem. It may be one or more of them, remember. In most cases, though, it is not all eleven! That would make it difficult to figure anyone out.

Remember what I said in the introduction about the bell-shaped curve. Most of us probably fall in the average part of the continuum on many of the traits that I discussed. There are a few of them, however, that we are undoubtedly either high or low on. It is these traits that cause conflict with people who are different from us.

When I have asked people to analyze problem bosses, co-workers, or subordinates in seminars, etc., we often begin by looking at differences in extroversion (many people say, "No, that is not a problem, we are both extroverts."), then conscientiousness ("No, we are pretty similar there."), and so on. Then we get to, say, the need for power, and the person says, "Yes! That's it. He must be very high in the need for power and I am low."

In this chapter, let's look at three examples of conflict at work: conflict among co-workers, conflict between an employee and a boss, and conflict between a new supervisor and her employee. In each case, the individual will use the questions and worksheet from each chapter to figure out how to deal better with conflict caused by the differences in personality, cognitive style, or communication style.

THE CANTANKEROUS CO-WORKER

Oscar looked up as his boss entered his cubicle and placed a glossy catalog on the desk. "Congratulations," said the boss. "Your five-year anniversary with the company is coming up next month. You'll be joining us at the anniversary luncheon with the others who are celebrating anniversaries next month, and you will also be able to pick out a gift from the five-year selection in the catalog here."

Oscar was left thinking about how fast time goes by. He enjoyed his job and almost all of his co-workers. The only problem, and it was a big one, was the co-worker a couple of cubicles down from his, named Hank. Oscar and Hank never seemed to see eye-to-eye on anything, and they had worked on several projects together over the course of the years. Oscar had gotten to the point where he dreaded having to go in to any meeting when he knew Hank was going to be present.

The last project the two were assigned to was a nightmare for Oscar from the beginning. It was a fairly simple task: Decide how to allot a large amount of grant money among several applicants. Hank, in Oscar's opinion, had taken an overly hasty view of the applications. He brought in a spreadsheet with some data about income level and need. Oscar wanted to talk more about the human beings behind the applications, but Hank didn't seem to feel any of that was important.

But then again, as Oscar looked back on this, he hadn't said anything at the time. He let Hank put his spreadsheets all over the table and take over the meeting. Oscar thought to himself that there was more to the decision than simply the data that

Hank had brought, but he had allowed Hank to overpower him. In fact, it wasn't until after the meeting was over that Oscar was able to think clearly enough to muster up arguments in favor of his point of view.

At the next meeting, Oscar tried to bring up his perspective. But he found himself not being heard. He tried more than once to interject a new direction to the team's agenda by saying things like, "What would you all think about . . ." and "Don't you all think it would be interesting if we tried . . ." When no one listened, he gave up. And he found it was usually Hank who got the team's attention away from him by saying things like, "Here's what we're going to do."

Oscar thought there were only three conflicting traits that described exactly what was going on with Hank and him. He marked the continuums to show where he felt he was (M for me) and where he felt Hank was (C for co-worker). Here is what he came up with:

Chapter 3: Venusians
Logical _____ C _____ M _____ Sensitive
Chapter 6: Martians
Compliant _____ M _____ C ____ Dominant
Chapter 9: Uranians
True Friend ____ C _____ M _____ Diplomat

Oscar then answered a few questions.

How do these traits help me contribute positively to situations?
I use feelings to make decisions, have a low need for power, and have an indirect communication style. That means I'm good at giving appreciation and support to other people. I'm a good collaborator and I'm cooperative and easy to get along with. I'm tactful and thoughtful.

When do I need to "stretch" a bit in the opposite direction?
I tend to avoid conflict, so I need to speak up a bit more and tell people what I am feeling when that is appropriate. I need to look at the data they bring to the table and think about the facts, not just my feelings. I need to voice my opinions more in meetings even if I need to practice my speech ahead of time and speak up before I

am comfortable doing so. I need to be a bit less tactful at times when I can tell I am not being heard.

How can I best call on Hank when I need to use his natural abilities?
Hank uses logic to make decisions, has a high need for power, and has a straightforward way of communicating. He is more effective than I am in some situations, which explains why he gets his point across better in meetings than I do. When he is on my side, that's great! Maybe next time we are on a project together, I'll meet with him ahead of time and tell him what I'm concerned about. That will appeal to his need for power. If I can get him on my side, he'll come prepared with the data in the spreadsheets to tell my story. And he'll be pushy and straightforward and powerful in the meeting, but he'll be doing it in a way that forwards my agenda.

Not only that, maybe I can learn a few things from him. I'll never be like him, but when something is important to me maybe I need to state it a little differently. Maybe part of the problem in that last project was the way I was trying to get my point across. I was a little too indirect, so no one listened to me. Not only that, I didn't even bring it up in the first meeting although something still could have been done about it.

How can I avoid expecting him to do things that fly in the face of his natural style? How can I stop being disappointed in him or angry at him when he does what just comes naturally to him?
Well, it's going to be difficult to just turn off my annoyance at him. After all, for the last five years I've seen him as the one thing that's been a problem about this job. But now that I understand our differences a bit more, perhaps I can remind myself to appreciate, and even come to respect what he's doing. I might even ask him to read this book. But I'm going to have to quit expecting him to change.

This is going to require some work on my part. And here I thought he was going to have to change. I'm going to have to tone down my values-based or emotional appeals when it comes to Hank or some of my other co-workers, who might be logical types.

How can I change my behavior to get along better with this person?
Maybe I'll have to look a bit more closely at his charts and graphs. I'm going to have to watch my tendency to give in, in meetings.

Even if I'm not giving in mentally, I'm sure not speaking up enough. I will need to learn to say so when I don't agree. And I need to think about how I say things. Perhaps I can take a lesson from Hank and those around me in how to be more straightforward in my communication. Some of those "We might want to think about" messages clearly are not getting through. Here I thought this was going to be about Hank! Turns out it's about me after all.

The next time some grant money came through for the organization, Oscar and Hank once again were asked to serve on the committee that allocated the funds. True to his plan, Oscar asked Hank if he could stop by his office the day before the first committee meeting. "Can I ask you about something, Hank?" Oscar began. "I know you've been around here a lot longer than I have, and I'd be interested in hearing your ideas. I know we've taken the same approach the last few times we've met on the grant allocations committee. I'm wondering about taking an approach where we can look at the people behind the application. What would you think about looking at things like their history, their backgrounds, the number of children they have; kind of a 'story behind the application' approach?"

"Oh, I don't know Oscar," said Hank. "It makes so much sense just to look at their finances and economic need. You can't really put any numbers on their life stories."

"You're absolutely right," said Oscar. "I was just thinking about something you said at our last meeting about how we tend to do things the same way all the time. You were right about that, and it might be interesting to take something new and exciting to the group tomorrow. They'd love it! What do you think? I know if anybody could put this into a spreadsheet you could."

"Well, let me see what you've got so far," said Hank, his attention caught despite himself.

Look what Oscar has done to this point. He is appealing to Hank's high need for power by letting Hank feel in charge, by agreeing with him, by saying things like, "If anybody can do it you can do it," making Hank feel like it was his idea. Oscar also referred back to something Hank said at the last meeting. Now let's see how the committee meeting goes.

Hank, of course, spoke up first. "You'll see that these spreadsheets look a little bit different from the ones you are used to seeing. Remember we were saying last time that we were getting tired of doing the same things the same old way. These are more detailed. Instead of just income and need these show a little bit more of the person behind the application."

Oscar began one of his prepared remarks. "These look great, Hank. I agree that it's time that we do something new. I've often thought that getting to the person behind the application is a better way to allocate the funds. What do you all think?"

"This is very different!" said one of the other committee members. "I'm not sure I like it. It introduces a lot of variables that seem a little fuzzy. I'm not sure we really want to get into all this touchy-feely kind of stuff."

Oscar, anticipating this, had another prepared speech ready. "I know that anything new is going to look a little strange at first. But let's take an opportunity to talk through this, because there are so many real merits of looking at it this way."

Wherever it goes from here, and it may or may not be 100 percent acceptable to the rest of the committee, Oscar has made a great start. He has found a way to work around his low need for power by coupling it with Hank's high need for power. He has found a way to overcome his compliant, diplomatic nature by preparing some of his contributions to the meeting ahead of time. He has made a start. He will have to keep practicing some of this behavior in meetings to come, but his next five years in the organization will be even more satisfying and productive than his first five have been.

MANAGING THE MANAGER

Charlotte was determined to enjoy every last moment of her Sunday evening. Monday morning meant going back to work, and tomorrow was the first day of her boss's return to work. "And I'll tell you," she said to her Pomeranian as she gave him a couple of dog biscuits, "the day Declan O'Brien returns to work is not a good day." He had been on an extended leave of absence for about three months. They had been good months for Charlotte, and she had enjoyed working for the temporary manager.

In the meantime, however, she had made some notes regarding the continuums of the characteristics in each chapter and only three seemed to apply to her situation. Here is what her list looked like, with M for "me" and B for "boss."

Chapter 4: Earthlings
Feet on the Ground _____ B _____ M _____ Carried Away
Chapter 5: Moon Landers
Isn't That Interesting? __ M _____ B _____ That's Wrong
Chapter 10: Neptunians
Big Thinker _____ M _____ B __ Stickler for Detail

Charlotte then answered a few questions.

How do these traits help me contribute positively to situations?
I am fun to be around and bring energy to the workplace. I react emotionally to things, so I am never boring. In addition, I am original, curious, and imaginative. I keep myself open to new ideas and new possibilities. I can think outside the box and come up with lots of new ideas. I like to look at the big picture.

When do I need to "stretch" a bit in the opposite direction?
I guess my emotions may make me hard to live with sometimes! People have told me I can be moody. I know I am sometimes impulsive. I have so many ideas that some of them are unrealistic. I get impatient when people don't see the merit of my good ideas as quickly as I do. People bogged down in details annoy me. So I guess I need to pay attention to some of their details.

How can I best call on Declan when I need to use his natural abilities?
Declan is calm, poised, and has the ability to control his impulses. I am used to interpreting this as him being cold, aloof, and uncaring. Maybe instead I can ask him what he's thinking or feeling. He also has a tendency to react to my new ideas and innovative thinking with killer phrases like, "We've tried that before and it never worked," or, "That's wrong." Maybe I need to give him more credit and look at that as him doing his job as the manager. Maybe he's being stable, reliable, and consistent like this book said. I need to figure out a better way to react by bringing in more facts and logic to back up my ideas instead of getting mad at him and just giving up.

He is also very detail-oriented. That's another way that he drives me crazy. When I come to him with a great idea, instead of getting excited with me he calmly says, "But what about X, Y, Z. . . ." It brings me down and I feel like never bringing him good ideas ever again. I guess I need to appreciate the fact that the details are necessary and quit expecting excited reactions from him.

How can I avoid expecting him to do things that fly in the face of his natural style? How can I stop being disappointed in him or angry at him when he does what just comes naturally to him?
This is going to be the hardest part. I think Jodie, on my team, is more like me. Maybe I can go to her ahead of time and show her my ideas and get excited with her. Maybe that will help, and I will get what I need from her in terms of reinforcement for my ideas. Then I will tell myself not to expect anything different from Declan. And I will not be disappointed when he reacts calmly. And I will remind myself that when he responds with a lot of detail, he isn't being critical. He simply doing what he thinks is helpful.

How can I change my behavior to get along better with this person?
First of all, I need to be calmer when I meet with Declan. He marked me down on my last performance review for being moody, whatever that means. So no matter what I'm going through that day, whether it's good or bad, I guess I need to "play a part" a little bit. I'll be like an actor in a stage play, and I'll play the part of "calm employee" when I'm going in to a meeting with Declan.
Second, because I know he's more fact-based than I am, maybe I need to approach him that way when I'm trying to convince him of something. I need to speak his language a bit more and either state things that way or ask him questions like, "What are the facts of the matter, as you see them?" I also need to look for ways that I can be of real assistance to him and help out when innovative, creative opportunities come by.
And last, I have to speak his language on the details. I can't just bring in big ideas and expect him to know what I'm talking about. Even if I don't know the path I took to get to the big idea, sometimes I have to create one in order for him to follow me. And here again, I can look for ways to help out when there's some kind of creative task that he can actually use my help on.

Monday morning has arrived. Actually, Charlotte wasn't dreading it quite so much because she had a plan. By Monday afternoon's scheduled staff meeting, she had the agenda for the meeting covered with additional penciled-in reminders to herself about her behavior in the meeting. She had done her homework!

One of the agenda items had to do with Declan requesting ideas from the staff regarding next month's annual fund-raiser. Ordinarily, Charlotte would have been the first to speak and would have been overflowing with tremendous enthusiasm and vague but big ideas. This time, she spent some time in the morning gathering some facts and figures that she knew Declan would respect. She also made sure that she was not the first to speak, but the second. She then said, "I have an idea for the fund-raiser that I think makes a lot of sense. One of our competitors did this last year, and it ended up raising a pretty good amount, as you can see from these figures I've prepared." She consciously spoke in a calm voice, and she passed around a sheet of paper with some figures on it.

Now, are you thinking that at about this time, Declan is wondering what alien beings have taken over Charlotte's body? I assure you it doesn't happen that way. Charlotte has made a couple of subtle changes to her behavior. She has calmed her response a bit, and she has brought some data to the table. She has moved a little bit down the continuum in a couple of her characteristics. Actually, her behavior looks just a little bit more normal to Declan than it used to. Chances are he is going to appreciate this, but it looks so normal to him that it isn't going to seem strange. He's going to like it. Notice that she isn't going overboard. She's moving in small steps. She isn't going to act like people who are on the far side of the continuum, but more like people in the middle.

Her next step may be to volunteer to be on the committee to implement this fund-raiser, where she can put her innovative, creative, "carried away" side to good use. She can also tap into the detail-oriented people on the committee to make sure that no details fall between the cracks. With any luck, her experience with Declan will lead her to appreciate those detail-oriented people and understand that she needs them on her side so that the fund-raiser is a success.

HARMONY IN THE WORKPLACE—OR NOT

The executive vice president was briefing all of the supervisors on some new policies and procedures. As one of the newer supervisors, Tamika was taking careful notes. At the end of the meeting, the executive vice president advised the supervisors to meet with their employees as soon as possible and go over the new policies carefully to make sure there were no errors in implementation.

On the way out the door, Tamika was chatting with her friend Larry. "You know, I was flattered when they promoted me to supervisor. But I'm not sure it's such a privilege. I'm not looking forward to this meeting much at all, for example. Most of my employees are okay, but there's this one in particular that's such a pain that it makes every meeting a chore and a bore, as the saying goes."

"Let me guess," said Larry. "Her reputation precedes her. Harmony, right?"

"I guess everybody knows about her," said Tamika. "I guess her mother had no way of knowing when she was christened, but her name sure doesn't fit her. She's just a disruptive influence at every meeting we have. She's like a black cloud hanging over everybody. She brings out the worst-case scenario of every idea anybody has. She hates any kind of new creative idea and comes up with dozens of reasons why it won't work. But when she's asked to serve on a committee to make it work, she's too busy or overworked. She's driving me crazy, and I've only been her supervisor for two weeks. She's a manager's worst nightmare. How do you deal with people like her anyway?"

When Tamika filled out the continuums, this is what she found (E is for "employee" and M is for "me").

Chapter 7: Jovians
Optimist _____ M _____ E _____ Pessimist
Chapter 8: Saturnians
Conformist _____ E _____ M __ Experimenter
Chapter 11: Plutonians
Self-Assured ____ E _____ M _____ Self-Critical

Tamika then answered a few questions.

THE BOSS FROM OUTER SPACE

How do these traits help me contribute positively to situations?
I am enthusiastic and generally happy, with a positive outlook on life. I have high self-esteem and a tendency to attribute good intentions to others. I trust other people and generally believe they are good. I am creative, I like to try new ways, and I value autonomy. I am ambitious, goal-oriented, and somewhat self-critical.

When do I need to "stretch" a bit in the opposite direction?
It seems I might view the world a little too positively. I might be taken advantage of when I trust people who don't really deserve to be trusted. As a manager, this includes my employees. I need to learn how to step up to the plate when I see substandard behavior from employees. I need to learn how to work with Harmony to let her know that her behavior in meetings is not acceptable. I've just been ignoring it for two weeks and that really isn't good management behavior.

Because I'm creative and like to try new ways, I'd better be careful with repetitive tasks. I may tend to let them fall between the cracks. According to the book, I don't really like standard operating procedures.

And because I'm self-critical, which means I'm a high achiever, I need to be careful not to assume that everybody else is like I am. It's okay to hold high standards, but I'd better do a reality check to make sure that the organizational standards match what I expect for the employees. I might have to be a little more patient with people like Harmony and not just think that she's a person of low standards.

How can I best call on Harmony when I need to use her natural abilities?
Harmony is more serious and realistic than I am. This is what I am experiencing as negative. This may be of value to me, because as I said above, there are times when I am too trusting and may be looking too much on the positive side.

Harmony is also someone who likes to plan the work and work the plan. I guess there really isn't anything wrong with that. I find it annoying because I'm more of an experimenter. I think what I need to do is find more tasks that fit her and delegate work to her that can tap into her organized, conscientious way of working.

She is also less achievement-oriented than I am. That's going be a harder one to deal with, I think. I'm going to have to quit expecting her to volunteer for things and delegate to her some of the mundane repetitive tasks that I find boring, and then I need to give her some praise and recognition for doing those things.

How can I avoid expecting Harmony to do things that fly in the face of her natural style? How can I stop being disappointed in her or angry at her when she does what just comes naturally to her? If my action plan in the previous section works, I should be able to gradually come to appreciate her more. After all, she'll be freeing me up to do more of the work that I enjoy, and she'll be working at her own pace to do some of the things that she is better suited to do. After all, pessimists, as Chapter 7 calls them, are pretty good at working independently, and I really don't have to watch over her shoulder. She should be pretty good at getting the work done once I carve out the work that she'll be good at.

How can I change my behavior to get along better with Harmony? I need to watch my interpretation of her behavior, or my misinterpretation, as it were. Because of our differences in the three areas that I've identified, I've been taking it personally when she acts in a way that I interpret as arrogant or unfriendly. She's just being a pessimist, but I'm an optimist. That's not going to change, but as her manager I certainly have the ability simply to give her work that is a better fit for her personality.

I also know that she's a conformist. I shouldn't expect her to act like I do in meetings. But I can't allow her to be a disruptive influence either. So perhaps I'll give her some advance notice when we're doing things like brainstorming new ideas and ask her to withhold her objections until after the meeting. Maybe she can take notes of her objections and present them to me in memo form afterward so that it doesn't disrupt the flow of new ideas.

And I know that she is what Chapter 11 calls self-assured and what I have been seeing as unmotivated. I need to recognize her achievements for what they are, not through my own high-achievement lenses.

A week later, Tamika sat down across from Larry in a booth at the company cafeteria. "I guess you're going to be my mentor in the Harmony situation," she said. "I've got to tell somebody, and because we started the conversation last week, you're elected."

"Sure," he said. "I forgot my newspaper today anyway, and I usually read over lunch. You can tell me your story instead."

"I knew I needed to meet with Harmony and talk about some of the things that were going on between us. But I didn't want a single her out, and I figured it was a good chance to meet with the other folks on my team as well. So I sent out a memo saying that because I'd been here for two weeks now, I wanted to meet with everyone individually to just talk about how things were going and how we could best work together effectively. Actually all the meetings were great. It was a good idea to have them, and I think all the employees appreciated it. But Harmony's meeting was difficult, although it turned out all right in the end."

"So tell me about it," said Larry.

"Well, you know, I knew that she tended to look on the dark side of everything, didn't like change, and wasn't really achievement-oriented. So I knew that she was going to tend to shoot down any new ideas that I had or that anybody else had. So I wasn't going to spring anything new on her in this meeting. And I was prepared for her to respond pessimistically to anything I said and I wasn't going to try to talk her out of that or become defensive. In fact, I had some responses prepared and jotted down where I could see them just to keep me from letting the conversation deteriorate.

"I thanked her for coming to the meeting with me, I thanked her for being a good employee all these years, and I told her I was looking forward to her being a part of my team because she had so much to contribute. She's been around and knows so much about the department. I told her that I'd noticed in the last couple of weeks that when people brought things up in meetings she had the ability to go right to the heart of what was wrong with issues. I told her that I appreciated that, but I felt that tended to bring the team down. And I gave her a couple of specific examples of times that she had done that. I told her that was an important role to play, but that it derailed the team meetings. I asked her if she could take notes instead and bring that information to me after the meeting so that together, she and I could take care of those details afterward. She seemed a bit flattered, actually, and agreed that we could do that and it would save time in meetings. I know this is only a start, but I think it's a good start."

I think you will agree with Tamika that she has made a good start with Harmony. With a pessimistic, self-assured conformist, you are dealing with an individual who has some pretty deeply ingrained personality characteristics and who is not going to change overnight—or perhaps even change much at all! But you can make some small changes in her behavior, such as the change Tamika is going to try to make to Harmony's behavior in meetings. Such small steps will make a big difference over time. They can be done, and Tamika's job as a supervisor will become much easier as a result.

NOW IT IS UP TO YOU!

Now it's your turn. Remember what I said in the introduction. Do you want to be happier, more successful, and more stress-free at work? I said that you only have to do two things well: get the job done, which I can't help you with here, and handle the relationships with the people around you, which I've done my best to help you with here. The rest is up to you. If you have a co-worker (or two) who is driving you crazy, or you've considered quitting your job because you can't get along with your boss, or you are the boss and your employees make you wonder if it's all worth it, follow my advice.

In the introduction, I suggested you do some Internet searches to find tests that will help you figure out where you fall on some of these characteristics. Pay special attention to the ones where you fall above average or below average. Those are going to cause you problems. People who score on the opposite end of the spectrum from you are going to annoy you in the workplace, but you need them. They see things differently than you, and together you make a good team. You need to understand and appreciate them, and the only way to do that is to overcome your annoyance and learn about them. So use the lists, use the techniques, and try one small step at a time, one person at a time.

 **Notes**

INTRODUCTION

1. John Gray, *Men Are from Mars, Women Are from Venus: A Practical Guide for Improving Communication and Getting What You Want in Your Relationships* (New York: HarperCollins, 1993).

2. Lucille Forer, *The Birth Order Factor* (New York: Pocket Books, 1977).

3. W. T. Norman, "Toward an Adequate Taxonomy of Personality Attributes: Replicated Factors Structure in Peer Nomination Personality Ratings," *Journal of Abnormal and Social Psychology* 66 (1963): 574–583.

4. J. M. Digman, "Personality Structure: Emergence of the Five-Factor Model," *Annual Review of Psychology* 41 (1990): 417–440.

5. Carl Gustav Jung, *Psychological Types (Collected Works of C.G. Jung, Volume 6)* (Princeton, New Jersey: Princeton University Press, 1971).

6. David Keirsey, *Please Understand Me II: Temperament, Character, Intelligence* (Del Mar, California: Prometheus Nemesis Book Co. Inc., 1998).

7. Daniel Goleman, *Emotional Intelligence: 10th Anniversary Edition; Why It Can Matter More Than IQ* (New York: Bantam, 2005).

8. Daniel Goleman, *Working with Emotional Intelligence* (New York: Bantam, 2000).

9. David Lewis and James Green, *Thinking Better* (New York: Rawson Associates, 1984).

10. John D. Gartner, *The Hypomanic Edge: The Link Between (a Little) Craziness and (a Lot of) Success in America* (New York: Simon & Schuster, 2005).

11. David C. McClelland, *Human Motivation* (New York: Cambridge University Press, 1988).

12. Patricia J. Addesso, *Management Would Be Easy . . . If It Weren't for the People* (New York: AMACOM, 1996).

CHAPTER 1

1. Greg Oldham, J. Hackman, and J. Pearce, "Conditions Under Which Employees Respond Positively to Enriched Work," *Journal of Applied Psychology* 61 (1976): 395–403.

2. Tony Alessandra and Michael O'Connor, *The Platinum Rule: Discover the Four Basic Business Personalities and How They Can Lead You to Success* (New York: Warner Books, 1998).

 **Index**

INDEX

INDEX

motivation, 180
motivational needs, 12–13

narrow-mindedness, 7
Neptune, 163
networking, by introverts, 20–21

Oldham, Greg, 26
open-ended questions, 29
openness to experience, 7, 84
opinions
    getting from compliant workers, 106
    taking responsibility for, 157
optimists
    characteristics of, 118–119, 127–128
    example, 117–118
    gaining balance, 124–125
    vs. pessimist, 115–116
    vs. pessimist, example, 204–208
    two working together, 119–120
    working with pessimists, 121
    worksheet, 129–130
orders, from boss, 159
organization, department image in, 189

paraphrasing, 111
people skills, developing, 27
perceiving, vs. judging, 132
perfectionism, 6
    and conformist, 134
performance reviews, from optimistic boss, 122
personality, 4
    factors of, 5–7
    Internet quizzes on characteristics, 15
    stability of traits, 121
personality conflicts, 14
pessimists
    boss as, 123–124
    characteristics of, 119, 128
    example, 117–118
    gaining balance, 125–127
    vs. optimist, 115–116

vs. optimist, example, 204–208
    two working together, 120
    working with optimists, 121
    worksheet, 129–130
physical energy level, 12
planting ideas with dominant worker, 105–106
Platinum Rule, 28
Pluto, 179
power
    as motivation, 12–13
    need for, 107
public recognition, 28

questions, open-ended, 29

recognition, need for, 180
reflectors, 35–36
    vs. actors, example, 37–38
    boss as, 42
    characteristics of, 38, 47
    gaining balance, 43–45
    interaction of two, 39–40
    interaction with actor, 40–43
    worksheet, 48–49
repetitive tasks, self-critical co-workers and, 185–186
reputation of disgreeing, 126
rules, experimenter view of, 135

satisfaction, internal, 11
Saturn, 131
self-assessment, 69
self-assured, 180
    boss as, 187
    characteristics of, 183, 191
    example, 181–183
    gaining balance, 188–190
    vs. self-critical, example, 204–208
    two working together, 184–185
    worksheet, 192–193
self-awareness, 10
self-confidence, 11
self-critical, 180
    boss as, 187–188